9 DAYS to Feel FANTASTIC

HOW TO CREATE HAPPINESS FROM THE INSIDE OUT

JOHN WHITEMAN
Creator of THE WAY

HAY HOUSE

HAY HOUSE
Australia • Canada • Hong Kong • India
South Africa • United Kingdom • United States

First published and distributed in the United Kingdom by:
Hay House UK Ltd, 292B Kensal Rd, London W10 5BE
Tel: (44) 20 8962 1230; Fax: (44) 20 8962 1239
www.hayhouse.co.uk

Published and distributed in the United States of America by:
Hay House, Inc., PO Box 5100, Carlsbad, CA 92018-5100
Tel.: (1) 760 431 7695 or (800) 654 5126; Fax: (1) 760 431 6948 or (800) 650 5115
www.hayhouse.com

Published and distributed in Australia by:
Hay House Australia Ltd, 18/36 Ralph St, Alexandria NSW 2015
Tel.: (61) 2 9669 4299; Fax: (61) 2 9669 4144
www.hayhouse.com.au

Published and distributed in the Republic of South Africa by:
Hay House SA (Pty), Ltd, PO Box 990, Witkoppen 2068
Tel/Fax: (27) 11 467 8904
www.hayhouse.co.za

Published and distributed in India by:
Hay House Publishers India, Muskaan Complex, Plot No.3, B-2, Vasant Kunj,
New Delhi – 110 070
Tel: (91) 11 4176 1620; Fax: (91) 11 4176 1630
www.hayhouse.co.in

Distributed in Canada by:
Raincoast, 9050 Shaughnessy St, Vancouver, BC V6P 6E5
Tel: (1) 604 323 7100; Fax: (1) 604 323 2600

Text © John Whiteman, 2012

Illustration p.17 © Luke Trickett, 2012

The moral rights of the author have been asserted.

A catalogue record for this book is available from the British Library.

ISBN 978-1-4019-4051-5

Collette, Finlay, and Mackenzie. Words can never express how I feel about you all... x

CONTENTS

Contents

INTRODUCTION

My intention in writing this book is to share The Way with you: The Way to bring more joy and happiness into your life; The Way to more contentment; and The Way to feel fantastic!

The Way is about you and how you feel. It is about taking where you are today in your life, and opening up more exciting possibilities and potential, so that you can live your life to its fullest extent. By taking small steps each day, you will be taken on a fabulous journey to a more energetic and fulfilled way of living that will stay with you forever. The purpose of this book is not only to get you feeling fantastic, but also to create a structure and an awareness that will allow you to self-manage how you feel, and create happiness from the inside–out.

The Way is a philosophy that evolved over my many years of working as a personal and business trouble-shooter, helping people to successfully overcome periods of adversity that were impacting both their business and their personal lives. During this time, I discovered that by getting people who were experiencing great hardship and stress to feel happier, my chances of then saving their company from collapse were greatly increased.

In order for me to understand a situation more, I felt that I needed to become deeply involved mentally, emotionally, and physically in a client's crisis: to know how they were feeling, and what I would do if I were in a similar situation. In essence, I became my client's partner – feeling their stress, experiencing their anguish, and living their ups and their downs with them. It was not always a particularly pleasant experience, but the desire to help them, and the challenge of saving their companies, drove me on.

When a company was in crisis I saw that a business owner usually had nowhere to turn for help, often losing friends and relationships in the process. I wanted to be there, to be able to dive in head first with my sleeves rolled up, and fight alongside the owner to save his or her company.

And this is how I led my life for many years, gaining knowledge from my direct experiences along the way. The downside to living a life involved with crisis management, however, does take its toll.

As each case finished, the release of pressure left me feeling exhausted and in need of recuperation. Many times, depending on the severity of a case, I became ill. But I felt that it was worth it to help people recover from being on the verge of losing everything, and seeing them confident and happy again was very rewarding.

One day, on the suggestion of my wife, Collette, who was concerned about me taking on all this stress, I decided to see if I could get my client to 'feel' better during their crisis, and so put them into a better mental state to save their company, while having less of an impact on me personally. To achieve this, I started to ask my clients to take certain actions, depending on what their emotional experiences were at the time. Client conditions ranged from anger, depression, anxiety, and marital problems, to lack of self-worth, and even suicidal tendencies.

When they were re-introduced to the elements that were lacking in their lives, everything just started to turn around for them. As they became happier from the inside their companies improved, and a positive impact was felt in their external lives as well.

I realized that I had a natural gift for seeing what was missing in people's lives and, by using my intuition, my clients started experiencing more personal happiness and contentment. This still allowed me to empathize, while staying more centered in my own energy. The more in touch I became with my feelings the more intuitive I became. I would sense an issue with a client, and then connect to their energy to feel what they were going through while being able to keep my energy raised. This gave me more clarity, and my intuition gave me the answers to their problems.

This is how I discovered that there were nine actions (elements) that consistently help people to improve how they feel. I put my findings into a philosophy, which has developed through finding solutions to people's life and business problems.

The 9 Elements are the foundation of this philosophy, which I call The Way. It evolved because I wanted people to have a simple way of regulating how they feel and moving forward with their lives. These nine simple actions are based on what was missing, and also out of Balance, in many people's lives. Once they introduced these elements, they became happier and more able to cope with their difficulties.

Over time, I began to realize that the special moments for me came less from saving the companies from crisis, and more from seeing my clients smile again – just to see the sparkle return to someone's eyes was priceless.

This book is about the 9 Elements and The Way to feeling fantastic.

PART I
Preparation

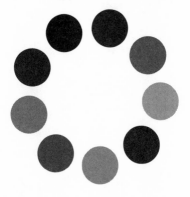

'Happiness is an energy you feel inside of you. When you feel good, life is good.'

ENERGY AND FOCUS

I would like you to take a few moments before reading any further to set out the intention of what you would like to gain for yourself.

I hope that you felt inspired to buy this book, and behind this inspiration was a desire. I would like you to keep hold of this feeling of inspiration and desire, so that you can keep the potential for growth alive. This is going to keep you motivated over the first five days, before the Momentum of the last three days starts helping you to create it naturally.

There are many great tools in this book and I know they have the power to help you to shape how you feel. The reason I feel so passionately about this is because I have already seen how they have worked for so many people. My desire is for you to start and continue to live the life that you have always dreamed of.

Our minds can be a great tool for development when they are consciously focused. If there is a loss of awareness and little direction, our daily thoughts can easily become negative, which causes us to be affected by our external conditions. This lowers our energy and stops us living life to its full potential. That's why I would like you to consciously focus your thoughts at the very beginning of this book on what your heart, body, and mind desires – not just your mind.

Your mind thinks in a linear fashion, but when you connect it to the whole of you – your mind, body, and spirit – an expanded way of looking at things comes about, bringing insights and solutions from within. You become centered and Balanced with the wisdom of your whole body. You will learn more about being connected with your mind, body, and spirit later.

But first, here is a little exercise to help bring you into Balance with the wisdom of your whole body. You can also listen to the free audio download by visiting http://thewayjohnwhiteman.com/9-elements-audio/ and entering the password 'Feel Fantastic.'

EXERCISE: Focusing the power of your intention

Start by focusing on the energy within your solar plexus (the area between your belly button and your sternum). You can place a hand there to bring more focus. Start to sense the energy and potential within you.

Quietly listen with your whole body to the power that is there. You can use the gentle rise and fall of your natural breath to keep your attention focused there for a few moments.

Once you start to feel this potential and power within your body, expand your awareness outward, toward the center of your chest and the base of your spine.

After a few moments, ask yourself: what are my heartfelt desires? Relax and let the answers float up through your heart to your expanded mind. Don't try to just think them, stay connected to your body and heart as well.

Throughout this exercise, stay connected to your heart. If you go from your solar plexus straight to your head and miss out your heart, you will be using your willpower only, which brings about energy that has strength, but lacks the ability to see the bigger picture. The energy of the solar plexus drives you forward, but lacks the wisdom of the heart. This forceful energy creates pushing, resistance, and tension in your body when things don't go as planned. So, maintain a relaxed state of being by staying in Balance.

YOUR POTENTIAL IS AMAZING

Your thoughts are like seeds in the fertile ground of your mind, body, and spirit. Let us take a few moments, now you are connected to your whole body, to prepare that ground by setting some intentions.

Why did you choose this book? What is it that your heart desires? You can write down your intentions if you like. I recommend you keep them in the present tense, as if they have already happened. For example: 'I am in Flow with life. I am healthy and slim. I am relaxed and calm. I feel fantastic. I am happy and full of joy. I am full of energy and feel that I can achieve everything that I was born to achieve. I see the potential in myself and other people. I am focusing on the positive things in my life. I am attractive and fun to be with. I am enjoying life.'

It might seem a bit strange to write your thoughts in the present tense, but it solidifies them in your mind as beliefs that are achievable and have the potential to 'be.' It is not just a future thought that stays as an unfulfilled desire.

CONSCIOUSLY CREATE THE LIFE THAT YOU DESIRE

Setting your intention stops the weeds of negative thoughts from growing – because you have planned what you want in your backyard – and having this clear purpose does not allow room for negative thoughts to grow. You have the power within you to be and feel fantastic. Thinking you don't have enough money to do what you want, or when you have lost weight you will find a new partner, or when you have paid off your mortgage you will fulfill your dreams are excuses created by your mind and they get in the way of feeling great.

It is all a matter of how you are thinking at any one time. You can wait to fully live your life by staying with negative mind chatter, or quash it with positive thoughts. You can choose fear and worry, or freedom and joy.

Creating awareness and raising your energy vibration is the key to feeling good.

9 ELEMENTS OF HAPPINESS

In choosing to read this book, you have given yourself a great opportunity to introduce the 9 Elements into your life. Once brought into your day, they will give you the tools to create happiness from the inside out. Within just 9 days, you will start to feel fantastic, healthier, happier, and more connected to your life. It's that easy. Some people might feel an automatic resistance against the idea that it is easy. All I ask is that you keep an open mind and come on this journey with me over the next 9 days and experience it for yourself.

To achieve this, we are going to introduce nine simple actions into your day; these actions are called the 9 Elements. A new one will be added each day, so that you gradually build all the actions into your day over the next 9 days.

The 9 Elements are designed to give you more Balance and Momentum in your life, and they will also help you to self-manage how you feel on a day-to-day basis.

The first five days will be about creating Balance, followed by three days creating Momentum, and then on the last day we will bring everything together in Element 9, which encapsulates them all.

These 9 Elements form the introductory framework of a philosophy I call The Way.

You can use the 9 Elements Diary on pages 227–238 to chart your progress and get in touch with how you feel each day. This will prove a valuable reference for you, as you begin to notice how the different elements make you feel over the next 9 days.

9 ELEMENTS OF THE WAY

The first step on your journey to feeling fantastic is to incorporate these 9 Elements into your everyday life. This is really easy to do, as if practiced regularly, they will naturally become part of your life. As with everything that is new, it might take a little change in the way you view yourself and your priorities. You may even feel guilty for spending more time on yourself, but when you feel good this feeling radiates outward and has a positive effect on all the people around you and your whole life. In turn, this lifts how you feel even higher. By the end of this book, you will have a way of managing your emotions whenever you need to. Just like a prescription for happiness. In fact, I have included a 9 Elements Prescription on pages 185–212 to help you see which elements are useful in certain life situations.

After only a short while, you will begin to gain awareness of how each one of the 9 Elements makes you feel. On the days you don't manage to incorporate them all, you will instinctively realize which of the elements you are missing. This is a great self-regulating habit, and a key benefit of the multifaceted way in which the 9 Elements and The Way work. Simply reintroducing the missing elements will help you to regain the Balance or Momentum needed.

We are made up of many component parts – heart, lungs, liver, etc. – all of which need to be functioning well, but people are often unaware of the energy that Flows through and within them. The 9 Elements help you to become aware of this energy, from the core of your body outward into the world around you. This new awareness will help you to be Balanced in your mind, body, and spirit as one, creating harmony and allowing you to connect with the energy of life that unites us all.

9 Days to Feel Fantastic is about you, your life, and how you feel. It will help you to get the most out of your life, and really enable you to start living the life that you have always dreamed of.

Life is full of potential, and by raising your energy you will find it easier to realize your full potential.

'Have you taken the time to feel the sun on your face today? It is these special moments we sometimes miss.'

CREATING SPECIAL MOMENTS

Life is created moment by moment. Practicing the 9 Elements is going to help you to create and notice the special moments in your life – the things that really matter. It is so easy to let special moments pass by unnoticed when we are caught up in our minds. Living life from a place of Balance and harmony helps you to register these special moments, and this registering raises your energy vibration further.

'When you feel good, everything is good.'

THE SCIENCE

Our current scientific understanding is that there are tiny vibrating spiral pieces of energy at our very core. As this energy becomes larger, we begin to perceive it as a solid form (matter or, in our case, the body) and it becomes 'you' and 'me' as we know them. In fact, you are an energy blob in a wrapper. Your internal energy impacts the environment around you. Like a pebble that has been dropped into water, its ripples radiate outward.

We will be using the Balancing and Momentum elements of The Way to get your energy vibrating at a higher frequency – one where you will feel full of life. You will be ready to see problems that might previously have lowered your energy as challenges, and this way of thinking will increase your energy even more.

*'It's not life that needs to change,
but the way we look at it.'*

When our energy is Balanced we have a more positive outlook on life and our life begins to Flow more easily. We begin to see endings as new beginnings and solutions instead of problems.

The 9 Elements will help you to feel happier, and improve your overall health by reducing stress, depression, and anxiety. You will learn how, just by making simple changes to your life, the 9 Elements are your way to the happiness that is inside all of us. You will learn to create happiness internally and radiate it outward, instead of from your external world inward.

Happy people have reduced depression and lead more fulfilled lives; they have improved health, reduced stress, and a more positive outlook. They have more energy and they have more fun. Happiness is not a creation based on your genes – which some people have and some people do not – it is a feeling inside you, which when nurtured radiates outward, affecting your whole life.

'Where your thoughts are, your energy goes.'

What we think about our beliefs and our emotions forms our energy vibration, which then determines the world we experience. We attract whatever is the closest match to our energy. If your energy vibration is heavy, and you habitually focus on the negative, that is how you tend to live your life. I am sure you have experienced times when your energy has been lowered by someone who is either in a rut or in a downward spiral of negativity. Having a raised energy vibration means these people will not affect you as much.

We are looking for you to raise the level at which your energy vibrates, so you will start to feel more positive and optimistic. Raising and improving the quality of your energy makes your thoughts, your emotions, and your life feel lighter because you start to attract higher vibration energy into your whole existence.

YOUR INTERNAL ENERGY AFFECTS YOUR EXTERNAL LIFE

The Way is about finding a Balance between your internal and external lives, as one is a reflection of the other. When your internal world is in harmony, your external world starts to replicate this effortlessly. I have seen my clients' lives turned around when their internal Balance has been restored.

For example, a client once came to me because he was very depressed and had little Momentum in his life. He was searching for a partner, but the more he pushed the more things just didn't go well for him. By taking action and restoring his internal Balance (days 1 to 5), he began to shine. By feeling better in himself he began to radiate more positive energy outward into the world and, by doing less and not searching as much, he found that not only had he become happy, but his energy was attracting a choice of partners. Now he is settled with a lovely person and enjoying a life in which he self-manages how he feels; he is living a life that Flows.

Sometimes this can cause people to feel strange, as they are used to doing and pushing all the time. When people's lives start to fall into place effortlessly they can even become fearful of it all suddenly grinding to a halt because they are not used to life being easy. But they often find that with less pushing they start to perform at a higher level. This is because pushing creates resistance, which creates internal tension within their bodies and their lives. When they let go of striving, but still keep the potential of something great manifesting, they experience relief in their bodies and their external lives start to Flow.

I am not saying that you won't come across challenges anymore but, as I said earlier, you will be able to view them differently.

BEING IN FLOW WITH LIFE

There is harmony between your internal energy and your external actions, and vice versa. Once you restore your natural Balance internally, it expands into your external life and creates the opportunity for Flow. By taking positive-focused action, you start to realize your dreams, creating Momentum, and begin to create the life that you have always wanted – one in which you get to reach your full potential, rather than just getting by and putting up with feeling just OK. When you are in Flow, you are in perfect harmony and are experiencing the state called enlightenment – you are at one with the source of life.

WHERE ARE YOU NOW?

I would like you to imagine for a moment your life as a river. At the beginning, your life starts at the source. Over time you move downstream, and gradually create your very individual journey until eventually you meet the sea. Along this journey there are many twists and turns.

Every river is different and every person's journey is an individual one. There are times when your river flows freely, and there are times when it slows down and becomes still.

There are clear times and cloudy times, vibrant and dramatic times, and then there are times when you just meander.

Now take a moment to picture your ideal river... flowing smoothly, changing direction whenever you need – you're having fun and your water is clear, fresh, and bright.

The 9 Elements of The Way are all about getting you to improve your personal river so that you feel fantastic.

In a non-judgmental way, take a few moments to think and feel where you are on your journey at the moment. Just bring some awareness to how your energy is Flowing today. Does it feel light, fresh, and vibrant or does it feel a little stagnant, dull, heavy, or flat? Is your river of energy expanding or contracting? Is it smooth and clear or rocky and turbulent? View your life as if it were a river.

The next 9 days will take you on a fabulous journey to a more energetic and fulfilled way of living that brings a fresh new perspective to your river, so that you can improve how it feels. In order to create this clarity, you will need to use the 9 Elements. Reading this book will only help you to understand how to make yourself feel fantastic. Experiencing the 9 Elements, however, will create a definite knowing that will stay with you forever.

THE WHOLE OF YOU

The 9 Elements work on the whole of you – your mind, your body, and your spirit. Many people spend a lot of time focused inside their heads, lacking the Balance that can be found in being in all three. By learning and using the 9 Elements, you will find that your life becomes richer as you begin to live in the whole of you, bringing your mind, body, and spirit into Balance. When you live from this Balance you respond instead of react to life – you see the bigger picture.

mind

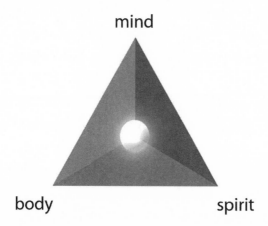

body   spirit

The 9 Elements are simple actions based on common sense, but we often only look at things in a linear, or one-dimensional, fashion. The 9 Elements give a multifaceted approach to feeling great from different directions; and it is by combining the different elements that you will feel fantastic. They also create self-awareness, which puts you in the driving seat of You and gives you the personal power to easily manage how you feel.

ONE STEP AT A TIME – JUST GO WITH HOW YOU FEEL

The Way is nonjudgmental. After following this book for 9 days, you will sometimes find that you cannot fit all the 9 Elements into your day. There will be some days when, perhaps, you only manage to include a few of the elements. Don't worry or be hard on yourself. Just 'be,' accept it, and know that you will feel better tomorrow if you fit some of the missing elements into your day. It's about Balance and noticing how you feel.

'It's not a race, more a connection with how you feel. Just notice how good you feel on the days you do all 9 Elements.'

ALIGNING YOUR THOUGHTS AND ACTIONS TO FEEL FANTASTIC

It is a good idea for your everyday thoughts and actions to become aligned with your intention. By doing this, you will reinforce the desire you have to 'feel fantastic,' and make it a priority in your life. With repeated practice, much like a tennis stoke, you will begin to bring this feeling into everything that you do. After you have practiced your stroke, you will become better at it and it will become second nature to you. Then it will be time to learn more – study another stroke or how to use slice or topspin. You will start to be drawn to what feels good, and which choices are aligned with how you want to feel.

Is what you are about to eat aligned with feeling fantastic? Is what you are doing for most of your day aligned with the intention you created for yourself at the beginning of this book?

By using this method of layered learning and introducing a new element each day, you will gradually achieve more Balance and Momentum in your life, creating change one step at a time.

WHAT I MEAN BY BALANCE AND MOMENTUM

Balance

Balance is the internal sensation you get when you feel calm and relaxed. This equilibrium provides emotional stability, calmness, and clarity, and allows you to act instead of react to situations.

When you have emotional Balance you feel centered in your being. In fact, Balance is all about being – being in harmony with the essence of life. Being in Balance allows you to see 'the bigger picture' and view life from a stable point.

Momentum

Momentum is positive forward movement that comes from taking action. It is the build up of energy needed to manifest your heart's desire. You are an expression of life, and Momentum is created from your passion to truly live this life. Momentum is uplifting and creates 'the wow feeling' – it's your natural stimulation, the feeling of excitement. When you connect with your passion, the build up of energy inside you propels you forward like a wave toward your intention. When you combine Balance and Momentum the feeling is fantastic. It is like you are surfing on top of the waves of life.

YOU NEED BOTH BALANCE AND MOMENTUM

My work as a business troubleshooter taught me that it is important for people to have both.

Balance on its own will not give you the happiness that you seek. You need the energy that Momentum brings, so that you can move forward and grow. Balance focuses you in 'being,' Momentum focuses you in 'doing.'

Too much stimulation and spark, especially if it isn't naturally created, can cause over-Momentum, which is very much like the feeling of running down a hill too fast. Extreme Momentum often causes you to fall over and burnout.

Being in Balance connects you to your spirit and Momentum gives you the ability to live your dreams. This, combined with Being Present, opens the door to experiencing the wonder and essence of all life.

'Be, then do.'

So let's get started...

9 ELEMENT TEST

We have created the 9 Element Test as a great way for you to check how much Balance and Momentum you currently have in your life. It will give you some guidance and a base point from which to start the 9-day program.

The 9 Element Test is a very short questionnaire that takes, on average, five minutes to complete. It can be found at: http://thewayjohnwhiteman.com/9-element-test.

It is not essential to take the test, but it will highlight what is most important for you to learn over the course of the next 9 days.

In taking this test you will gain knowledge about which areas of your life need more attention. Your responses to the questions will give you an overall 9 Element Test score, and a score broken down into three sections:

- Balance
- Momentum
- Being Present

It is a good idea to make a record of your score, so that you can compare the results by taking the test again at the end of the 9 days.

Your 9 Element Test score:

Day 1
Overall Score ....
Balance ....
Momentum ....
Being Present ....

Day 9
Overall Score ....
Balance ....
Momentum ....
Being Present ....

Thousands of people have taken this test anonymously, and we have some statistics later in this book which confirm how beneficial the 9 Elements are to people in improving their day-to-day experience of life, and in helping them to feel great.

'When you know where you are, it's easier to know where you are going.'

PART II

Balance to Momentum: 9 Days to Feel Fantastic

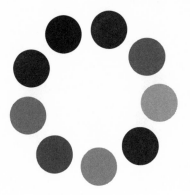

'Happiness is not about what you have got, it is about how you feel inside.'

EXERCISE

Element 1 is EXERCISE, a Balancing element.

'We are born to move.'

This is one of my favorite elements, because there is nothing that raises your energy faster than exercise. Exercise decreases your stress hormones and increases endorphins – the body's natural feel-good chemicals – so your mood is boosted naturally and automatically through exercise. Or in simple terms, it makes you feel great.

It is only relatively recently that we haven't exercised naturally as part of our typical day. Our earliest ancestors were concerned solely with survival, which relied on being able to catch food, move from place to place and, when necessary, running away. Exercise affects how our energy feels: mentally, physically, and emotionally.

A river that doesn't move stagnates. Much the same happens to us if we don't move – the less we move, the more this impacts on how we feel. Exercise is going to get your energy moving, raise your vibration, and give you more zest for life.

The Way philosophy centers on energy; it is at the core of us and plays a part in everything we do.

THE POWER OF POSITIVE THOUGHT

The hardest part of moving is to go from a sedentary state. Once you are moving, however, your body settles down, gets into a rhythm, and your energy begins to Flow.

So, I would like you to focus on noticing how good you start to feel after you have done some exercise, rather than on the resistant feelings that are there because of some stagnation before you get moving. You know – that sluggish, bored, unmotivated feeling you get after a day or so of chilling out and doing very little physical activity.

Focus on the thought:

'I want to feel fantastic and moving my body will help me to do just that.'

Many of us have been conditioned to think of exercise as 'Oh no! I have to go to the gym,' or 'Oh no! I have to get fit.'

Well, actually, you don't.

You don't have to do anything you don't want to do. The choice is yours.

We often have negative thoughts that sabotage our best interests and offer excuses not to exercise. I would like you to let go of those thoughts and focus on feeling full of energy, happier, and enjoying life as much as you can.

If you don't take any action, your energy will continue to feel sluggish and heavier than if you had exercised in some way. So, if you really want to feel fantastic, moving will get your energy feeling higher, creating that buzz for life.

For me, morning is the best time to exercise, only because barriers and excuses tend to get in the way throughout the day. If I exercise first thing it allows me to feel its positive effects throughout the rest of the day.

The way to get motivated to exercise is to actually do it. The best type of exercise for improving your mood are cardiovascular: exercises that raise your heart rate, such as running, fast walking, cycling, swimming, and dancing. It is this vigorous type of exercise that helps your body to release the endorphins necessary for a mood-enhancing high.

USE THE POWER OF INTENTION

I would like you to align your thoughts with your actions and make feeling fantastic your priority over the next 9 days. Reading this book, following the exercises in it, and applying the information to your life.

Over the next 9 days you will be caring for yourself in a way that shows you think your wellbeing and growth is important and worthwhile. It is an exercise of self-care, because how you feel is important to you.

Maybe your desire is not to have anger and frustration, or chaos and drama in your life. Or perhaps you just want to feel good. Whatever your intention, allow this willingness to change to drive you forward.

So if you want to feel strong, healthy, and full of energy – and let's face it, who doesn't want perfect health – then you need to match your thoughts with your actions.

When you feel tired and have no energy, this can sometimes be a great time to exercise, because it will create some of that energy you desire. This could then lead you to become more active in your social life – having more fun with friends, or even making new ones with a new hobby. Or your new hobby could be exercise based, such as martial arts or badminton with family or friends – anything that gets you moving and is fun.

Look to teach yourself:

*'If I have no energy and I exercise, it will
give me energy and make me feel good.'*

It's that simple. If your energy is depleted and listless, exercising will make you feel better and fitter. You just need to make that commitment to yourself to improve how you feel. If your tiredness is due to medical reasons, though, this is best checked by a medical professional before you start any physical activity.

So today I am asking you to exercise for between 20 and 30 minutes.

Yes, 20 to 30 minutes. That's only 20 to 30 minutes in a day of 24 hours.

If you only manage between 10 and 20 minutes, that's

fine too. It's not a race. You just need to get moving. All of the Elements of The Way are about You, and getting you to feel fantastic. So if you incorporate exercise into your day, you will notice an immediate change in how you feel. This will then spur you on to keep feeling good.

'The benefit is your health, and the positive improvements to your life are massive.'

HOW FIT ARE YOU?

The first step is to assess your fitness, and to go at a pace that suits you. If you have not exercised for a long time, are overweight or have any medical conditions, it is essential to contact your doctor or a health and fitness professional before starting any exercise program.

On our Spa Days and Workshop Retreats we gear exercise according to people's abilities: Moderate, Active, and Advanced. I am looking for you to gradually build up your level of exercise to become fitter and get your energy Flowing.

Moderate range

If you are moderately fit, start exercising gradually with either brisk walking or light jogging, or perhaps try dancing, yoga, or tennis. Like a car, the hardest part is getting going so find something that feels like fun –

you will be more likely to keep it up. Finding a friend to exercise with is also a great way to keep motivated on those days when the television and sofa are calling you. It is more important to build up progressively, rather than over-stress your body and put yourself off exercising because of overly sore muscles, so just do what feels right for you.

If you are not used to going to a gym or running, formal exercise might feel a bit daunting. Whereas participating in a fun activity, where you are not trapped in negative thought patterns about exercise, is a good idea, as your mind will become engaged completely in doing the activity, rather than listening to negative thoughts that stop you from carrying on.

You'll always feel better *after* exercise than before, because physical activity stimulates various brain chemicals that make you feeling happier and more relaxed than you were before you worked out. You also look better and feel better when you exercise regularly, which in turn can boost your confidence, improve your self-esteem, and help prevent depression. Exercise also has the added benefit of reducing frustration and anger.

Only you know what is the right amount for you. Please don't do too much too soon. It's easily done. Your aim is to find and use the tools of The Way so that you can self-manage how you feel. So start gradually and connect with your body – that way you will not push yourself too much.

Active range

In this range you will feel comfortable running, or, alternatively, doing some other form of aerobic exercise. Exercise at a level that gets you perspiring and breathing faster, but at a rate where you can still hold a conversation. We want to stress and stimulate your body, but not overly so.

I have found over the years that exercise helps people with anger, depression, and, to a lesser extent, those suffering from anxiety and sleep problems.

Advanced range

In the advanced range you will be accustomed to taking daily exercise, and I would like you to adapt your level to suit you. The maximum level I have found comfortable and sustainable is about two hours a day, before it becomes too much of a stress on your system. See what works for you. We are generating energy to feel good but, because of its feel-good factor, exercise can become addictive and over stress your body.

HOW MUCH EXERCISE DO I NEED?

No single element is the answer to creating Balance and Momentum. However, if you are suffering from anger, depression, anxiety, or sleep problems, perhaps ask yourself these questions:

1. How often do I exercise? When we're busy we often let exercise lapse from our day-to-day life.

2. How do I feel after I have exercised? Hold on to this positive feeling and imprint it in your mind, so it is stored there for when you might need to remember how good exercise makes you feel.

3. At what level did I exercise? Is it getting too easy for you? Or are you doing too much?

These questions are designed to give you more awareness of this element in your life.

TURNING NEGATIVES INTO POSITIVES

Let's take just one emotion: Anger.

Anger can be used as a positive emotion, as long as it is vented constructively. Anger is the extension of frustration and, if directed in the right way, it can bring about the action that is needed to stop it building up. This means staying connected to the whole of your body. Your mind on its own lacks Balance and tends to cause you to resist anger, holding on to it and delaying you from finding a solution or a positive vent. Your mind also has many thoughts and beliefs about what should and shouldn't happen. In both cases, when you feel anger or frustration building up, you will find that movement helps to Balance this emotion. Exercise connects you back to your body and literally shakes anger out of you. Try it and see for yourself.

It is important to allow your emotions to Flow: anger and frustration are a build up of unreleased energy. Like a kettle on the boil, pressure builds up until it needs to be released. Finding a way of positively letting off steam can propel you forward. A positive view is that the burst of energy that comes from frustration and anger can empower you to achieve amazing feats, which, if your energy has been low, you could not have previously imagined.

For example, during divorce many people feel angry that their marriage has failed, but they find this anger then propels them on to doing things they would not have done if they were still in the relationship. It becomes a time for growth.

GETTING MOTIVATED

A common problem with people starting and maintaining daily exercise is a lack of motivation. It is so easy just to sit in front of the television, or to put it off by doing something else instead. One thing I would like you to be aware of is that Motivation comes from Action, and not usually the other way round. Action creates the energy, which creates more motivation. So you need to Do it first. In doing so, your motivation will increase.

So, once again, when you have the least energy, this is exactly the time that exercise will help you create more energy.

If you are the type of person who hits the pastries and chocolate bars mid-afternoon, then this is the best time to exercise. Why not drink some water (dehydration can often be a cause of tiredness or feeling hungry) and go for a brisk walk, or run round the block a couple of times instead? This will kick-start your energy, and align you with feeling fantastic. Again, try it and see for yourself. By experiencing the positive results, you will be inspired to continue to incorporate the 9 Elements into your life.

. . . .

Actions for DAY 1

Exercise for 20–30 minutes.

So come on. Get those running shoes on. Get ready. The best time to do something is NOW. I know you want to start feeling fantastic as soon as possible, so let's get moving and take a positive step toward feeling fantastic.

How are you likely to feel?

By the end of Day 1, I would hope that your energy is moving a bit more around your body, and that you are feeling a little fresher and lighter, calmer, and have more clarity. Depending on the extent and intensity of your workout, particularly if you haven't exercised for a while, you might have found the exercise itself a little slow and possibly that your mind was wandering and playing a few tricks. If this is happening to you, look to feel what your body needs rather than what your mind is thinking. Whatever exercise you choose, you should engage your breath and your body completely.

If you take exercise already, I am sure just by exercising today you will feel good for doing so. Getting your energy moving and finishing not only with a sense of achievement, but also the feel-good factor that is created by exercising.

You might notice a few creaks and groans as your body gets moving. Your mind might be giving you negative signals to stop or to slow down, or even to give up, as it is too hard. Sometimes there is a barrier to go through as you start anything new. After breaking through this barrier you will find a natural rhythm. Rhythm is the objective. Rhythm followed by Flow. Allow your body, and not your mind, to give you signals.

One easy way to understand whether the signals are coming from your mind or your body is to notice your breath. Aerobic exercise will create active use of your breath. If your breath is being actively engaged, then your thoughts are on your breath and this is good.

The next step is to notice your pace. Too fast and you over-stress your body, and the signal you get back is breathlessness. This will cause you to stop quickly to restore Balance because you have pushed too much. Too little exercise and your mind will wander. If this occurs, increase the intensity and bring your mind back to your breath.

Notice the positive changes you experience before and after exercise, and how these connect you back into life, creating a feeling of aliveness and increased energy Flow.

• •

That's it for Day 1. Good luck and enjoy yourself.

DAY 2

PERSONAL SPACE

Element 2 is PERSONAL SPACE, a Balancing element.

'Five minutes each day just to "be."'

I hope you managed to exercise yesterday. If not, there is always today. Exercise is a key part of The Way, and that is why it is Element 1.

Today we are going to introduce you to Personal Space. Having some personal space, or 'you time,' is very important, and often gets overlooked in our busy day-to-day lives.

Many of us don't take time to STOP – we always start each day in a rush to get things done, and are always thinking ahead to what we need to do. But if we can stop 'doing' for five minutes a day, preferably in the morning, I find that the whole day changes for the better. You have more clarity and a sense of being more in charge of your life. Your breathing is more relaxed, which in turn causes your muscles to relax, and you will be more focused on what needs to be done, rather that chasing your tail all day, leaving lots of things unfinished.

Does this happen to you sometimes?

This is how many busy people lead their lives, and it shows how important personal space is for a more Balanced and enjoyable life.

Let's take a moment to see what a difference these five minutes of just 'being,' rather than 'doing,' could make to your day.

You could spend five minutes connecting to your breath. This will help you to connect with your body more, creating space to settle your mind so your thoughts come from a more centered place within. This quality is then carried with you throughout the whole day.

RUSHING

Many people get up at the beginning of each day and start 'doing' straight away, which creates a rushing feeling that leaves them tripping up throughout the rest of the day. If we are not centered, we are not conscious of what we are doing.

So we can't remember where we put our car keys or our phone, because our actions are not conscious. This can lead to a chaotic life and increased personal stress.

Most people live in their heads. They over-analyze things, worry, and have endless mind chatter. In fact, the way we are going, what do we need a body for now? Just to carry our head around! Maybe in a couple of million years we might evolve into a head with a couple of feet sitting underneath, so let's start connecting with our bodies as well. By connecting your mind, body, and spirit you become whole. You respond instead of react to life from a more Balanced place within.

'Just "be."'

Element 2 of The Way is about being, not doing, and in those moments of stillness you have a chance to become aware of your body and spirit (the essence within you), as well as your mind.

As you connect more with your body, you may start to notice that your shoulders are raised and your teeth are clenched, or other areas where you are holding tension. It is useful to breathe into these areas. Taking five minutes each day to stop will allow you to realize how you feel: whether you are tired, stressed, depressed, or ready for a new challenge. If you don't stop and create awareness, how will you know what effect your life is having on you?

If you find you like this element and are gaining great benefit, you could extend the time to 10 minutes. Perhaps, if you are feeling a bit overwhelmed, you could add another period of personal space into your day, or perhaps in the evening to help you wind down before you go to bed.

It's all about Balance. Balance will create a calm state within your body, so that you can observe your life unfolding and be able to make better choices rather than reacting from habit.

USE YOUR BREATH

Look to use your breath to calm your mind and connect to your body. We are not taught how to breathe because our body does it naturally and unconsciously. But when we encounter stress, or feel fear, we tend to hold our breath or breathe shallowly. This way of breathing creates tension within the body and causes us to hold on to our energy in those areas.

If you would like to know more about ways you can use your breath, try a CD I've created called *Breathe*, which teaches ancient breathing techniques in a contemporary way. This can be found at http://thewayjohnwhiteman. com. You can also listen to the free audio download by visiting http://thewayjohnwhiteman.com/9-elements-audio/ and entering the password 'Feel Fantastic.'

Breathing exercises have been found to be effective in reducing anxiety, depression, irritability, muscle tension, headaches, poor concentration, and fatigue. Oxygen is the most important chemical in the body. It's amazing to realize that your body removes 70 percent of its waste products just by breathing. Also, our brains use 25 percent of all the oxygen we take in, and the average person takes in 21,600 breaths per day.

Over the next eight days, take five minutes of personal space just to be with your body by focusing on your breathing and your senses. This short amount of time just allowing yourself to 'be' can make a big difference to how you feel throughout the day.

Here is an exercise that you can read and then do afterwards. Even better, as you focus on your breath, you can listen to the free audio download created for this book at http://thewayjohnwhiteman.com/9-elements-audio/. Just enter the password 'Feel Fantastic'.

EXERCISE: Connecting with your breath

Find a comfortable space where you can have five minutes to yourself. Preferably with a view of nature – even some houseplants or a view of the sky will do. You can start by either sitting or lying down – whichever feels better for you. Your eyes can be closed or open, and your body simply relaxed.

I would like you to follow your natural breath in and out of your body. Feeling the air at your nostrils as it goes in, and then as it travels to the back of your throat and down your windpipe to the very base of your lungs, and then back out again with a nice even breath, no forcing. Take two to three breaths.

Notice the natural feeling of letting go as your breath leaves your body.

Notice that the air is slightly cooler on your inhale and warmer on your exhale.

If you choose to keep your eyes open, you can connect and breathe with the nature around you, as if you and nature are one. This can be both calming and energizing.

So, just keep your focus on your breath going in and out. You can even say to yourself in your head as you are breathing in and out:

Just breathing in... and out...

Just breathing in... and out...

And then simply:

...in... and out...

...in... and out...

This helps you to focus your mind on your breath. It is usual for your mind to start wandering, so don't worry about this, just recognize when it does and bring your focus back to your breath.

...in... and out...

...in... and out...

And continue for the next three or so minutes.

Now bring your awareness back to the whole of your body, and to where you are sitting. If your eyes are closed, open them slowly, and take a few moments to connect back in with your immediate environment. Wriggle your fingers and toes, stretch your body, and take a few moments to see how you feel.

Well done, that is five minutes of Personal Space finished. Enjoy the calmness and clarity that it brings to the rest of your day.

EXERCISE DAY 2

How are you feeling today?

Hopefully you got your energy moving yesterday. Today I would like you to exercise again.

Most people who regularly build exercise into their lives do it once, twice, or three times a week. What I would like you to consider, whenever possible, is to include exercise into your daily life.

You can make it a gentle form of exercise, like going for a relaxed walk if you are feeling a little tired, or a more vigorous type of exercise if you have lots of energy. Sometimes you won't be able to find the time with everything else you might be doing in a day. But on the days that you do have time, you will have more energy reserves to help your mood and positivity, and this can last for two or three days. It is worth noting here that it is a good idea to notice how your mood changes with the absence or presence of exercise.

So let's do it. Let's make your life a more energetic one, where everything is possible. One that gives you the ability to manage and control how you feel on a day-to-day basis. On days when your body tells you it needs a rest, don't exercise. But on most days, just vary the activity you do so that you use different muscles to avoid over-stressing the same ones. If you want to gain all the benefits from exercise, however, not just the mood-improving aspects, you should do at least 20 minutes of moderate exercise every day.

One way I monitor whether I should exercise or not is by taking my resting pulse when I wake up in the morning. That's counting how many beats your heart does in a minute. If you notice an increase of two or three beats, either don't exercise or do less, as your body may be fighting off an infection. Keeping a regular routine is what you're looking for – one that gives you the feeling of wanting to exercise. This will happen when you are more in tune with what your body needs.

DRAGGING AND DRIFTING

When people join gyms and health clubs, they always have the best intentions – to get fit and healthy, to look and feel good. Often other things get in the way, though, and they get sidetracked. In The Way this is called Dragging and Drifting.

Dragging is where something or someone is pulling you in a different direction than what is best for you. You get a heavy feeling and it doesn't feel great.

Drifting is where you become distracted, or have too many things on your to-do list, and end up steering off-course and not achieving what you intended. As with all plans, it is important for you to stay on-course with the 9 Elements. You will find, as each day unfolds, the build-up of improvement will help you to get closer to your goals.

If you managed to exercise yesterday, your body will already be experiencing a movement of energy rather than a feeling of stagnation. If you enjoyed the after effects you should be feeling better. You are now moving toward an improved and healthier life. Well done.

. . . .

Actions for DAY 2

The new element for today is Personal Space.

- Personal Space: just five minutes, stopping and focusing on your breathing.

- Exercise: 20–30 minutes, getting your energy moving around your body.

How are you likely to feel?

Depending on your starting point, the feelings and emotions you will be experiencing on Day 2 are likely to be varied. What I would love you to notice is how you felt at the start, and how you feel after each completed day – and not just the feeling of 'I'm out of breath ☺,' more your internal feelings. Am I feeling calmer? Have I less frustration? Am I smiling more internally as a result of exercising and personal space? Use the daily diary at the back of the book to keep a record of your feelings each day.

. . . .

Enjoy your day.

DAY 3

SLEEP

Element 3 is SLEEP, a Balancing element.

'Create clarity in your day.'

N ow that you have brought two essential elements of
The Way into your life – Exercise and Personal Space
– you are beginning to layer the foundation that will help
you to bring more awareness and energy into your life.

You are also doing things that will make a massive
difference to how you feel, and this will also have a positive
effect on everyone around you.

Do you sometimes wake up feeling groggy? Spend
most of the day with a foggy head, unable to concentrate
on what you are doing, perhaps making silly mistakes?
These unbalanced feelings could mean that you need
more of Element 3: Sleep. There is a direct correlation
between lack of sleep and stress, anger, anxiety, sadness,
and your ability to cope.

A variety of different things can help you get a better
night's sleep. Developing a regular wind-down routine
is one of the most important. A pre-sleep ritual acts as
a cue to your body that it is time to sleep. This might
consist of a warm bath, listening to relaxing music, or
using your breath to switch off your mind, and relax your

muscles. It is a good idea to keep vigorous exercise to the daytime, or early evening, because its energizing effects can prevent you from sleeping. We are looking to create rest and relaxation. A time for your body to stop, recharge, and repair itself for the following day.

HOW MUCH SLEEP DO YOU NEED?

On average, most adults need between seven and eight and a half hours of uninterrupted sleep a night. Good-quality sleep, where you are actively dreaming (REM sleep), will improve your concentration and help regulate your mood. Lack of sleep can make you irritable and cranky, affecting your emotions, social interaction, and decision-making.

Everybody is different, but if you wake up feeling well rested and refreshed you are getting the right amount of sleep. Another important key to a good night's sleep is to keep your bedtime routine consistent. If you vary the time you go to bed by a great amount, this will have a knock-on effect the next evening, causing you to get into a cycle of not getting enough sleep.

For example: If you go to bed late one evening and sleep late the next morning, you might not be tired at a reasonable time in the evening. If you then stay up late but can't lie in again, then your sleep is cut short. If your sleep patterns are irregular, the quality of your sleep is affected. In respect of the 9 Elements, just be aware that if you have not managed to have a good night's sleep, it is natural that it will affect you. Sometimes there can be a delay of a couple of days before your mood is impacted. So just become aware of how you feel, and what is missing from your life in a non-judgmental way, and you will know why. You will understand what has caused it, be able to catch up over the next few days, and then feel better.

DEVELOPING A GOOD NIGHTTIME ROUTINE

Today I would like you to take some time to wind down at the end of the day. Switch off the television earlier than usual, or stop any stimulating activities earlier in the evening than usual.

Allowing yourself enough time to unwind will help you to let go of your day, and prepare for sleep. It is best to avoid bright lights in the evening, as well. Bright lights at nighttime stimulate your mind, and delay the increased release of melatonin that your body puts into your system, which affects your Circadian rhythm and the desire to sleep.

If you like to read in bed make it something that is relaxing. If a book is a real page-turner you might find that you can't stop, so set yourself a time that you would like to go to sleep to give you seven to eight and a half hours of sleep, and then stick to it. Sleep helps to organize memories, solidify learning, and improve your concentration.

Sleep well.

EXERCISE DAY 3

Do 20–30 minutes.

Today, once again, I would like you to exercise while also being aware of how you feel. Don't push yourself too hard. Go inside your body with your mind and use your intuition to feel what your body needs. You may want to do more today if you feel that you have more energy, or a little less if you feel tired. The important thing is to get moving; our bodies are designed to exercise. If you take time to look after yourself, you will be rewarded with a strong, flexible, healthy body.

Just do 20 to 30 minutes of exercise today. You can move your body in any way you like: playing football, taking an exercise class, or having fun with your children in the park. Maybe go swimming or biking. Variety will keep you motivated, and make it easier and more enjoyable to fit activity into your day.

It is important to warm up and stretch your muscles before exercise, as stretching prevents aches and pains and promotes the health of your muscles, tendons, and ligaments. There is no better time to stretch than Now.

Look to include a pre-exercise and post-exercise stretch into your day, allowing your body to warm up and cool down. If you have tight muscles, try connecting your breath to the muscles you are stretching, while gently holding the stretch without straining. Straining causes more tension. Take yourself to the point where you start to feel the tension, and then come off a little and focus on relaxing all the muscles in your entire body, even your face. It is amazing how much tension we can hold on to without realizing it. Exercise is a good way to connect with your body – notice how it feels.

PERSONAL SPACE DAY 3

Our focus today is sound.

Personal space can be as easy as taking time out to sit somewhere quiet, where you won't be disturbed, with a cup of tea. It is just about taking time to 'be' rather than 'do.'

We are going to focus on a different sense each day. Today we are using sound.

I would like you to find a comfortable place to sit down, somewhere you will not be disturbed. The best place to do this is out in the environment, or as close to nature as possible. The best time is whenever it suits you. I find that it works best for me at the very start of the day, just before the hustle and bustle of the world has got going. It is a magical time when you are less likely to be disturbed, and it is also a time when you can almost feel the energy of the day slowly gathering.

We are now going to spend our five-minute Personal Space time focusing on sound. You can do this exercise now, or later while listening to my free audio download. Just visit http://thewayjohnwhiteman.com/9-elements-audio/ and enter the password 'Feel Fantastic.'

EXERCISE: Focusing on sound in your Personal Space

Let's begin.

Make sure you are in a comfortable position, seated or lying down with your eyes closed, and in a place where you won't be disturbed.

I would like you to listen to the sound of your natural breath. Don't force it – just see if you can hear the sound it makes as it flows in and out through your nose.

As you identify the sounds, take care not to create thought patterns related to those sounds. Stay in the listening mode. The idea is to direct your thoughts and mind, rather than react to your surroundings.

Just listen to your breath as it goes in… and out…

While listening to your breath, let your natural breath gently fill your lungs and travel all the way down your body to about an inch below your navel, and gently out again.

As you breathe in, allow your tummy to expand with air and, when you release the breath, notice it and allow it to drop.

Just listen to the sound of your breath coming in… and out… in… and out…

Now I would like you to become aware of the sounds that are close by. If your mind wanders, just bring it back to your breath, and the sounds that you can hear. Not processing or analyzing, just listening.

Bring your awareness to the sounds a little further away from you... breathing in... and out...

And now the sounds in the far distance... breathing in... and out...

Now notice all the sounds, near and far, together. Feel the energy of your environment... breathing in... and out...

Begin now to gently bring yourself back to where you are sitting, and take a few moments to reconnect with your immediate environment.

Wriggle your fingers and toes.

Take a few deep breaths...

Slowly open your eyes and stretch.

Take a few moments to see how you feel.

Well done, that is Day 3 over – enjoy the calmness it brings.

Actions for DAY 3

The new element for today is Sleep.

- Sleep: Wind down gradually over the course of the evening.

- Exercise: Just 20–30 minutes a day.

- Personal Space: We are focusing on sound as the sense for today.

Just by taking some time for yourself you can change not only how you feel, but positively affect the people around you. Have a fantastic day.

How are you likely to feel?

Most people will be feeling more Balanced emotionally from the breathing and relaxation exercises, and possibly a little tired if they have actively been keeping a good aerobic pace with exercise.

Sleep is important for rejuvenation, so please set aside some space and time today to bring awareness to this element and how you feel on Day 3.

DAY 4

NUTRITION

Element 4 is NUTRITION, a Balancing element.

'Fuel yourself with the energy your body needs.'

Almost halfway there – fantastic! By now you will already be starting to feel fitter and healthier; you will also have more emotional Balance.

These first five days are about bringing more Balance into your life and getting your energy moving.

The more often you bring the 9 Elements into your everyday life, the more you will instinctively become aware of whether you need more Balance or Momentum. By knowing this – and it does change, just like your moods change daily – you will begin to harness a better quality of life for yourself. A life in which, when you feel a certain way, you will just know which elements are missing. Then, by re-introducing those elements, you will restore your mind, body, and spirit to the optimum Balance and Momentum that is needed.

Today, on Day 4, we are going to cover the fuel that gives you energy and helps you to feel fantastic.

In The Way we recommend eating food and drinking water from as close to the original source as possible. We are all aware that it is important to have a healthy, balanced diet that contains lots of fruits and vegetables, and moderate amounts of protein and carbohydrate, but the quality of what you eat, and how you eat it, is equally as important.

THINK 'FRESH AND LOCAL'

The best possible source of food is one that comes from growing your own vegetables, picking them and putting them directly onto your plate. This food will be the very freshest possible because it has taken the shortest distance to reach your table, and has therefore lost the fewest nutrients.

After growing your own food, give some thought to where the next source of fresh food could be. This could be your local farmers' market, or neighborhood or farm shops that stock locally grown, seasonal produce. Food without pesticides and chemical fertilizers is naturally kinder to your body. I like to choose organic, free-range products whenever possible. Wherever you shop, look for where your food has come from. Eating poor-quality food definitely has an effect on how you feel.

It is helpful to become aware of how many vital nutrients are lost from food during packaging, transportation, and storage. Food that is sourced locally is almost always fresher, as it comes to you directly from nature with the least delay. This is food that has not been chilled, packed, and flown from the other side of the world before reaching your table. Food picked when it is ripe, rather than being picked prematurely and ripened without sunlight.

You connect more with your food and have a completely different buying experience if you get to meet the people who have grown and harvested it. This is why I enjoy buying food from a farmers' market so much; the stallholders are passionate about their produce. They love telling you what time they picked their produce – sometimes it is that very morning.

THE QUALITY OF YOUR FOOD CAN AFFECT YOUR ENERGY LEVELS

Today I would like you to become aware of every piece of food that you eat or drink, and ask yourself the following questions:

- What is the quality of this food that I am about to eat?

- Where has this food come from?

- Is this food going to give me good, healthy energy?

- Is it aligned with wanting to feel fantastic?

- Would something else be a better choice for me?

- How will my body feel once I have eaten it?

This will really help you to connect with what you are eating and help you to make better choices.

A simple way of doing this is to rate what you are choosing to eat with a score out of 10.

So, just before you eat something, think out of 10:

- What is the quality of this food? How good is it for me? How will my body feel once I have eaten it?

In fact, you can try this rating process with everything you eat, drink, and do. Then listen to your body:

- Does my body really want this food?

- How far has this food traveled to get to me?

- Is this food aligned with feeling fantastic?

- Is what I am watching on television aligned with feeling fantastic?

- Does this activity score a 10, or a 1?

BECOME AWARE OF YOUR BODY

The first step to eating more healthily is to become aware of what your body needs, what energizes you, and what fuels your cells to perform at the level at which you want to perform. I am not looking to tell you to do something, because 'telling' creates resistance. Rather, I am suggesting what will help you to feel fantastic, enabling you to become aware of how you feel so you can decide what makes you feel good and become aware of how you can self-manage how you feel.

When a craving comes into your head for something that is not aligned with feeling fantastic, use your breath to connect with the whole of you – your mind, body, and spirit – and then ask yourself:

- What does my body need?

- Is this just a habitual craving that is covering up another need? (For example: the need for more Balance, rest or self-care.)

- Is there a better choice?

Take a few moments to decide, or maybe do something else for half an hour and see if the craving passes.

THE IMPORTANCE OF READING LABELS

When looking for food that is as close to nature as possible, it is helpful to take a look at the list of ingredients in the product you are buying. Try to buy food that has the smallest amount of additives possible. Food additives are substances added to food to preserve or enhance its taste and appearance. They can be of natural or artificial origin.

I have compared two drinks for you: a typical orange drink and fresh orange juice. Here is the list of ingredients for each item.

Fresh orange juice

Ingredients: 17 oranges.

Orange-flavored drink

Ingredients: Water, Glucose-Fructose Syrup, Orange Fruit from Concentrate (10%), Sugar, Citric Acid, Preservatives (Potassium Sorbate, Sodium Metabisulphite), Acidity Regulator (Sodium Citrate), Natural Flavoring, Sweeteners (Aspartame, Saccharin), Stabilizer (Cellulose Gum), Natural Color (Carotenes).

The high-sugar, low-fruit content of the orange-flavored drink might not come as too much of surprise to most people, as the difference in quality between fresh orange juice and flavored drinks is well known. But what is surprising is the amount of food additives that flavored drinks contain.

Try to eat natural food as often as possible. Food with fewer additives, the way nature intended food to taste and not a manufactured taste.

Simply, eating food that is as close to nature as possible is a good way to ensure you are feeding yourself healthy food. You can argue that fresh orange juice is more expensive, but at the expense of what? Is it your wallet, or your health? Filtered water would be a cheaper and much healthier choice.

A tip for reading food labels

Ingredients are listed in order of weight, which means that the main ingredients in packaged food always come first. This means that if the first few ingredients are high in fat, sugar, or refined carbohydrates, this food is best eaten only in small amounts.

From today onward, look at what you fuel yourself with, and how it makes your body feel. There is a high correlation between what you eat and how you feel.

EXERCISE DAY 4

Exercise again for 20–30 minutes today.

Exercise helps you manage your weight because when you exercise, you burn calories. The more intense the activity the more calories you burn, and the easier it is to keep your weight under control.

Once you have completed the 9-day program, you will begin to notice how your mood and energy change whenever you do or you don't exercise. See if you can feel the energy shift and change in your mood today before and after you have exercised.

It usually takes two to three days of not exercising for you to notice that your energy is starting to feel sluggish.

Finding the time to exercise

You can fit exercise into your life in many ways. You might like to go for a walk during your lunch break, although don't forget to take time to eat a healthy lunch as well. Do jumping jacks, sit-ups, and press-ups during commercial breaks while watching television. Or even better, switch off the television and go for a run. You could jump on your bike or walk briskly to make a local journey instead of using the car. The physical activity you accumulate throughout the day helps you to burn calories, and adds to your energy levels. It also turns exercise into a healthy habit.

The pace that I find is most beneficial to exercise is one where a moderate sweat is created, and where I am totally focused on doing the exercise in question, whether this is running, tennis, mountain biking, or karate. When you are 'in the zone,' you switch off from everything else and nothing else matters. This is a great way to manage daily stress, as it gives your mind a rest and brings your awareness back into Balance.

Getting started off is the hardest part. Once you have, after a short while (for me it is about 20 minutes when I run) you will find your mind switches off and you move more into your body and your spirit (by connecting with your breath). It is only when this mind, body, and spirit Balance is created that you are positioned to move into and experience Flow.

This is Day 4 and you have come a long way already. You are using your body in the way it evolved to be used. Fantastic, well done!

PERSONAL SPACE DAY 4

We are going to focus on another of your senses, and today it is sight.

Find a comfortable spot to sit down – this can be as easy as sitting on your lawn or the deck with a cup of tea, or perhaps in a park, but preferably in a natural environment and somewhere you can have a moment of peace.

Find a place just to be. Just to notice what is going on around you with calm observation.

Take in your environment. Look out and see the colors surrounding you, observe the shapes. Take in objects close to you to start with, and then increasingly further and further away. Then bring everything you see in together.

Slow down, and take a few moments to notice the detail and texture in what you see: the small things that usually go unnoticed in a typical day – perhaps a spider's web or a dandelion seed floating in the wind. Notice how nature is in constant Flow, and take note of the variation in shade and depth in the objects you see. Watch birds in flight. Just feel at one with your surroundings. Try not to label and analyze the things you see, just 'be' and let everything just come and go with quiet awareness.

If you feel the temptation to start thinking about your day ahead, or something from yesterday, just bring yourself back to the present moment. You could try connecting with your breath, as a subtle way to connect with your body and inner self, rather than your mind. This can really connect you with the essence of the objects you are looking at, rather than mentally giving them a label.

Breathe in the colors, shapes, and textures, and look at your surroundings with fresh eyes, as if you were a young child seeing them for the first time... and just be.

I have seen massive improvements in people's lives when they do this element alone. With the hurried lives that many of us lead these days, taking time for personal space can help us to stop rushing. It also helps to connect you with your more intuitive and creative side, as well as Balancing your emotions.

Each day we will be connecting with one of your senses to bring you into the present moment. When you are present, your perception of time will also slow down because your attention is focused in the moment rather than always searching ahead for the next thing. When you stop searching for a better moment, you start to see how beautiful life is already.

SLEEP DAY 4

Winding down to sleep.

With sleep today I would like you to follow a similar pattern to yesterday: allowing yourself time to wind down in the evening. But today I would also like you to avoid any caffeine or sugary drinks after midday.

This will be easier for some than others; it is all about Balancing how you feel. Some people live with extremes of mood and energy swings, so eliminating sugary drinks and caffeine after midday can help to break this pattern. If you feel a slump in energy and you would usually reach for caffeine, ask yourself 'Why do I feel this way?'

People find themselves in a vicious cycle in which caffeine contributes to sleep disturbance, but then, because of the sleep disturbance, they feel tired and want more caffeine.

Try not to cover up your body's messages with a stimulant. You could be feeling tired because of a physical cause, such as anemia or an underactive thyroid, or an emotional cause, such as stress and worry, or because of your lifestyle. Are you dehydrated? What you eat and drink can have a big impact on how you feel. Alcohol, like caffeine, is a drug that can lead to a cycle of tiredness. Some people drink alcohol to help them to relax and sleep, but alcohol can disturb your sleep cycles. You may get your eight hours, but because your quality of sleep has been reduced, you still wake up feeling tired.

So today try to make the best choices of food to fuel your body and, most importantly, always listen to your body first and your mind second. That way your thinking will be connected to the whole of you.

Actions for DAY 4

Nutrition is the new element for today.

- Nutrition: Become aware of the quality of food you eat. Is it aligned with you feeling fantastic?

- Exercise: Do 20 to 30 minutes again, remembering to stretch and listen to your body.

- Personal Space: Focus on the sense of sight today.

- Sleep: Avoid caffeine or sugary drinks after midday.

How are you likely to feel?

If you have managed to keep up, and have completed all of the days and elements so far, you should be feeling fitter, and have more clarity and awareness in each day. Your energy will definitely be becoming more Balanced and calmer.

You might also find it a little strange that your increased awareness means you begin to see people and situations in a slightly different light than before. You are possibly becoming more objective, less judgmental, and less confrontational.

ENVIRONMENT

Element 5 is ENVIRONMENT, a Balancing element.

*'Your environment
impacts how you feel.'*

Your everyday environment has an effect on how you feel. You resonate with the vibration of the energy that surrounds you. Whether this is at work or at home, the geographical area where you live, the weather, the sun, or the moon, all of these factors have an impact on how you feel.

I would like you to take a few moments now to notice whether your immediate environment feels positive or negative. Is anything noticeably affecting you? Is anything or anyone affecting your mood? Is there anything that is creating tension or a feeling of lightness in your body? Are you enjoying or resisting your surroundings. Even smells can make a difference to how you feel.

The environment is one of the Balancing elements, but it is also a bridging element as it can create both Balance and Momentum in your life depending on how you choose to use it.

For instance, being in nature usually feels Balancing, while a city environment can often feel more stimulating. In this book we will be using the Environment as a

Balancing element, as most people need more Balance, rather than Momentum, in their busy lives.

In a natural Balancing environment you feel as though you are being soothed. Your shoulders drop as tension is released, and your energy begins to settle down. This is why people often sigh when they experience the calming effects of nature.

In a city environment, on the other hand, Momentum is created as your energy starts to resonate with the Momentum of a fast-paced environment. The busy and rapidly changing manmade sights and sounds around you stimulate your senses. After a while this stimulating environment can become draining, as you get caught up in a fast current of energy that contains little Balance.

THE BALANCING EFFECTS OF NATURE

Being outside in the natural world is a very positive and Balancing environment. I would like you to start to spend more time each day in a positive energy environment: one that refreshes you and gives you energy rather than sapping it from you.

Sometimes, changing a heavy or stagnant atmosphere inside a building can be as simple as opening the windows, or using sound to change the vibration of the environment. Music is an easy way of lifting the energy vibration in your body, and you can do this by playing music, humming, or even singing. Many cultures use singing and chanting to focus the mind and lift the spirits. The rhythmic sound of people chanting at a soccer game creates an energetic atmosphere, uniting the supporters and players. In turn, the players' feelings are lifted by all the support, which has a positive effect on how they perform.

Where can you go today to be in a pleasing natural environment – one that will help keep your energy feeling really good? Maybe you can eat your lunch under a tree in a local park, or on a bench, feeling the sun on your face? Even if you are out walking in a busy street, try focusing on what is positive in your environment. If all you see is straight, manmade lines, and gray concrete, try to switch your focus on to the beauty in life. Notice the people who are smiling, the shapes of the clouds in the sky, a tree blowing in the wind, or some wonderful architecture. You might be able to hear someone laughing. It just takes a little more awareness and a change of focus to become conscious of the beauty that life presents to us every day.

Creating awareness helps you to stop and feel the wind on your face, and connects you to your internal and external environment. It is so easy to get caught up in your mind and trudge along with your head down, thinking about what you need to do next rather than connecting to your life as it is happening now, how you are feeling, and what effects your surroundings are having on you. Being more aware of your environment gives you a chance to notice and seek a better one, or to become aware of changing your thoughts about the one you are in.

Spending some time in a natural environment today will not only help you to Balance your emotions, it will connect you to the beauty surrounding us all that we sometimes miss.

EXERCISE DAY 5

Do 20–30 minutes, exercising in a way that suits you.

Today I want you to consider bringing the environment into your exercise time. Why not get out in the fresh air and go for a run or a brisk walk, and feel the wind in your hair and on your skin? It is uplifting to be outside, moving your body, being playful and having fun. If you live in the city, you could go to your local park, or jump on a bus, travel in your car, or bike to somewhere new. It is refreshing to get out into nature and explore. You could try a new type of exercise today, or something that you did when you were a child, such as skipping, basketball, or trampolining. Connect with the benefits of exercise, breathe in some fresh air, and enjoy yourself. That way exercise will become part of your day without it feeling like a chore.

From now on, I would like you to manage your exercise routine based on how you feel.

If you are finding your exercise fairly rhythmical and easy, this is often a signal that you need to stimulate your muscles and mind by varying your exercise routine. How about upping it a bit today? It is good to encourage a bit of stress back into your system for you to grow once more, and feeling positively challenged keeps it exciting.

Using exercise to manage your emotions

The best form of exercise for me is running. It's not that I love exercise, it's the feeling it gives me afterward that I love. It spurs me on to do it again the next day. I have found that exercise helps my clients to reduce stress and create Balance in so many emotions – depression, anxiety, anger, insomnia, self-worth, clarity, etc. In fact, doing some exercise each day will help Balance most of your emotions.

Whenever I have a client who is very focused in their head and finding it hard to see a clear way forward, I take them running with the sole purpose of exhausting them. (I only do this with people who are medically fit – I would not recommend you do this unless you are already exercising and have a clean bill of health.) I find this is a great way of helping them connect with their breathing and their body. At some point they stop thinking externally about their life, because the exercise means they can't focus on anything other than how their body is feeling and their breathing. It brings them into the present moment and out of their minds, creating clarity and awareness as frustration and mind chatter disappear.

Once, as I was giving a talk, a woman in the audience who had suffered from depression for many years suddenly had the realization that everybody has all the emotions within them. For many years she had thought that she was the only one experiencing all of these emotions.

We all experience all of the emotions: the key is to spend more of your day experiencing and recognizing the positive ones. This is achieved by using the 9 Elements to raise your energy vibration, which will align you with higher thoughts. Put simply, practicing the 9 Elements softens the resistance in your body and allows your emotions to Flow through you. Practicing them also Balances your mind, body, and spirit because negative thoughts, which cause negative emotions, are formed only in the mind; you simply view them from your center rather than allowing them to affect your body.

I have personally felt and seen how these tools can help people to manage their emotions and live a much more Balanced and happy life.

'We all experience all of the emotions: the key is to spend more time experiencing the positive ones.'

For many years I held on to my emotions about negative situations that had occurred in my life. This is what many people do to one degree or another. Holding on to negative emotions for a long period of time, however, can have an effect on your health, as does holding on to positive emotions: they both manifest energy, positive and negative.

For some reason we tend to let go of the good emotions quickly, so I thoroughly encourage you to allow your emotions to Flow, and to begin to create a habit of focusing on the positive ones instead of the negative ones. This is done by not engaging with any negative thoughts – witness them in you, but don't pick them up.

> *'We can only hold one thought at a time, so if you don't give something your attention it just falls away.'*

We have a fun element to learn tomorrow.

> *'Make the most of your day today because what you do today will affect how you feel tomorrow.'*

PERSONAL SPACE DAY 5

Today we are going to focus on your sense of smell.

For Personal Space today, when you wake up, look to come into your day gradually.

This might mean getting up a little earlier than usual, but it will be worth it to feel fantastic. Allowing your body to wake up gradually will help you to start your day from a calmer, more centered place.

Today we are going to focus on your sense of smell and if you can practice this outside in a natural environment, even better. Notice the smell of the flowers, the wind, and the grass – everything has its own unique fragrance.

Consciously connecting with your immediate environment will heighten your sense of smell. You could go for a relaxed walk in a natural environment, or notice what you can smell as you make your first drink of the day. Using your senses connects you to your environment through your body instead of your mind. It keeps you centered and present.

By focusing on one sense each day, you will begin to heighten each of your senses individually. About 80 percent of what we taste is actually due to our sense of smell, and I am sure you have noticed how bland food tastes when you have a blocked-up nose or a cold. Take some time today to notice how your food smells, and see if your enjoyment of eating is heightened as a consequence.

SLEEP DAY 5

Today we are going to learn to switch off.

With sleep today there is a choice, and this choice will depend on how much energy you have left toward the end of the day. You can add in another gentle exercise or a personal space session. Both will be very mellow and about you becoming more relaxed. For exercise, try perhaps 5 to 10 minutes of gentle stretching, or some yoga-style postures. For personal space, you could focus on your natural breath as we did on Day 2. Both will allow your mind to become quieter and enable your muscles to relax.

Follow this with your new wind-down routine at bedtime. Have a warm bath, a cup of herbal tea, perhaps read a relaxing book. If your mind is racing with things that you need to do, or if you are stressed about something, one way of getting your problems and worries out of your head is by writing them down before you go to bed. Knowing that they are released and stored somewhere else creates the space for sleep to happen naturally. Focusing on your breath is very helpful, too, if you are finding it hard to switch off your mind.

NUTRITION DAY 5

For nutrition today we are going to focus on water and hydration.

Water is the most important nutrient in our bodies. We are made of about 70 percent water, so being dehydrated really does affect both how we feel and our performance. Now that exercise is becoming part of your day, it is even more important to stay hydrated. If you only drink when you are thirsty, this means that your body is already in a state of dehydration. Some effects of not drinking enough water are tiredness, dry skin, headaches, and reduced mental ability. If you don't take in enough fluid it is also harder for your body to get rid of waste, which can lead to constipation and other intestinal problems. If you are dehydrated your body will take fluid from non-vital tissues in order to send it to vital organs like the heart, brain, and kidneys. If this becomes a long-term situation, it can have a serious effect on your health.

Most of us don't drink enough water in a day to meet our body's most basic requirements. Today I would like you to start drinking at least 3–4 pints (1.5–2 liters) of water a day, and more if you live in a warm climate or are exercising strenuously. Try to carry a bottle of water with you at all times, and get into the habit of sipping it throughout the day. Drinking little and often will help your body to retain and use water more effectively.

Drinking water can also help curb your appetite and raise your metabolic rate. Adding more high water content food to your diet will also help increase your level of hydration. For example, fruits and vegetables have naturally high water content, as does food that absorbs liquid during cooking, such as rice and oats.

Metabolic rate

Your metabolic rate, also know as Basal Metabolic Rate, is the rate at which you expend energy at rest. If you have a low metabolic rate you will have a tendency to burn calories off at a slower rate and be more likely to store any excess as fat. An increased metabolic rate will have the opposite effect.

There are many contributory factors – including diet, age, sex, exercise, and weight – that have a say in our individual rate, but maintaining a consistent exercise plan and a healthy diet will increase your rate.

So let us hydrate to feel fantastic.

. . . .

Actions for DAY 5

The new element for today is Environment.

- Environment: Notice how your environment makes you feel.

- Exercise: Do 20–30 minutes.

- Personal Space: Tune into your sense of smell today.

- Sleep: Try adding a relaxing stretch or another personal space session into your wind-down routine.

- Nutrition: Remember to drink 3–4 pints (1.5–2 liters) of water a day.

How are you likely to feel?

You are now at the end of Day 5 and will have completed all of the Balancing elements. You are likely to be feeling much more emotional Balance than when you started on Day 1. A calmness and reflectiveness will start to grow inside you, and this will positively affect your ability to handle day-to-day situations.

At the time of publication, over 3,500 people have taken the 9 Element Test. Of the people who are incorporating the five Balancing elements into their day, more than 86 percent either feel good or fantastic. I hope at this stage, on Day 5, you are beginning to as well.

Tomorrow we will start to introduce you to the first of the three Momentum elements. The Momentum elements will feel slightly different to the Balancing elements, as they will begin to ignite the spark within you.

How far have you come?

Take a moment now to remember how you felt on Day 1 and compare it to how you feel today.

How are you feeling today, and what changes have you noticed since you began? Write your answers below.

_____

_____

_____

_____

_____

_____

_____

· ·

ACHIEVE AND COMPLETE

Element 6 is ACHIEVE AND COMPLETE, a Momentum element.

'What are dreams for,
other than to be lived?'

E lement 6 is one of my favorite elements. For me, it encapsulates what life is all about, and that is really living and doing the things that excite and inspire us.

It is great to have Balance in your life, but Balance without Momentum is like having a fabulous sports car on the driveway that doesn't get driven. The Balance that you have created over the last five days will give you a great foundation. Now you can move forward by using the Momentum elements of The Way.

CREATING MOMENTUM DAY 6

Achieve and Complete is about positive forward movements, which most of us enjoy and are what keeps life exciting. We need some 'get up and go' in order to live those special moments, experience life, and do the things we have always wanted to do. It helps if you know where you are going, as it allows you to create focus and avoid drifting.

Goals create Momentum and stimulation. Why not do something spontaneous today? Do the things you have always wanted to do. It can be something small each day, or build up to something big in the future – completion is the key. Ticking a goal off your list every day will give you the satisfied feeling of having achieved something. It really lifts your mood and your whole day. It could be as simple as making a phone call that leads you one step closer to achieving a dream!

We are often busy rushing around, trying to do lots of things at once, but not actually completing any of them. This leaves us feeling exhausted and frustrated, because nothing is getting completed. If you focus on one thing at a time, you gain focused Momentum with each achievement; this then starts an almost effortless Flow of getting things done.

Flow is the movement that occurs when you get your energy moving in a positive way without any forcing. Pushing to get things done creates resistance. When you have Balance you are more centered and able to enter a state of Flow more easily.

EXERCISE: Becoming inspired

I would like you to take some time today to write a list of at least 10 special things that you have always wanted to do. Perhaps taking a yoga holiday, climbing a mountain, running a marathon, writing a book, or learning to dance. It is about doing positive things in your life to make it feel like you are really leading the life you want to live.

Think of things that you will look forward to achieving, and which you will also enjoy completing.

Tap into your heart's desires and connect with all the things you have always wanted to do. What inspires you, what gets you thinking, 'Wow, wouldn't that be something fantastic to do?' This list can contain small, medium, or large dreams. Just allow your feelings to Flow.

I once had a client who, when I asked him to do this exercise, looked at me with a tear in his eye and asked if it was OK to do it. He felt guilty about spending time on himself, doing something he wanted to do. He thought his needs weren't important, but, of course, they were.

Life is an experience for all of us to enjoy. Maximizing the positive aspects will lift you and allow you to do more of the things you have always wanted to do. This then encourages and inspires other people to live their dreams. Not truly living your life doesn't help anyone. In fact, always looking after others at the cost of your own joy can lead to unhappiness and nobody wants to be looked after by someone who is unhappy. So do something for yourself and set a good example for the people around you. Living The Way is about being and doing. So just be and just do. Enjoy writing your list!

My Dream List

1. _____

2. _____

3. _____

4. _____

5. _____

6. _____

7. _____

8. _____

9. _____

10. _____

11. _____

12. _____

13. _____

14. _____

15. _____

EXERCISE DAY 6

Exercise for 20–30 minutes.

Why not set yourself some exercise goals: short, medium, and long term.

Start with something simple and then think of something totally awesome that you could achieve in the future. If you make your goals realistic they will become more achievable. In addition, if you have a fantastic goal and break it down into a series of mini goals, you will also make it become more achievable.

If you are fairly new to exercise, consider these goals:

Short-term goal: Jog to the next lamppost and then walk to the next two for as long as 20 minutes.

Medium-term goal: Walk briskly or jog for 30 minutes.

Long-term goal: Complete a 6-mile walk or a half marathon. If you are active or advanced, how about taking part in a triathlon or a marathon, or climbing a mountain?

The list of exercise goals is endless. Maybe you want to learn to flamenco dance, or row a set distance in a set time, or get a black belt in a martial art, or do a back flip. The choice is yours.

> 'Everything is possible in your life
> if you take one step at a time.'

In getting out there and doing it, you will know it's not about *believing* that you can do something, it is knowing you can do it and then experiencing it, which heightens life's richness.

My recommendation for people who are not in the active or advanced range would be to exercise with a friend, keeping the intensity of an activity at a level that creates perspiration, but still allows you to have a conversation without becoming breathless. This will stop you from going too fast too soon.

So, have fun and feel the energy Flow through your body.

PERSONAL SPACE DAY 6

Feel and touch are the senses for today.

I am now going to introduce you to an exercise that will help you to become aware of what you can feel on the inside of your body and on your skin.

This personal space session will last five minutes. You can follow along with the words as you focus on what you can feel, or read the exercise first and then do it by yourself afterward. You can also listen to the free audio download by visiting http://thewayjohnwhiteman. com/9-elements-audio/ and entering the password 'Feel Fantastic.'

EXERCISE: Increasing awareness of your Personal Space

Let's begin. Make sure you are in a comfortable position – seated or lying down with your eyes closed – and that you will have no distractions.

Bring your awareness to your breath, without trying to change it.

Feel the cool air as it enters your nasal passages.

Feel how your chest and abdomen rise and fall as your breath enters and leaves your body.

When you attempt to follow your breath you may find that your attention wanders. If you notice this happening just gently bring your mind back to the breath again.

Now let's bring your awareness to your muscles.

Can you feel any areas of tension in your muscles?

If you can, breathe into those muscles and see if you can let go of any tension on each breath out.

Now let's take your attention to the energy of your inner body.

It can be very subtle – just keeping your awareness on your inner body is enough.

Can you feel any areas of stagnation?

As before, breathe into these areas, placing your mind and your breath there...

Now take your awareness to the surface of your skin and the points of contact you have with the things around you.

What can you feel?

Can you feel a breeze on your skin?

Or maybe the warmth of the sun?

Or the fabric that is touching your skin?

Now take your awareness to the area 2–3ft away that is surrounding your body.

Can you feel your energy radiating out from your skin and mixing with your surroundings?

Bring your attention to the space about 5ft from your body. Notice the space in front of your body, at the back of your body, to the right and left of your body, and above and below your body. Connect with your breath and breathe into this space. Notice what you can feel.

I would like you to slowly draw your awareness back through the space surrounding your body and back to your skin, feeling your dense body. Once again, become aware of yourself and the points of your body that are touching the floor.

Your personal space time is coming to an end.

Wriggle your fingers and toes.

Take a few deep breaths in… and out…

Open your eyes slowly and stretch.

Great, now you have completed Personal Space for Day 6.

While still having an intention to manifest your desires, bring the 'just being' that you experienced in your personal space time into the rest of your day and watch it unfold without any pushing or attachment to the results. That way your day will just Flow.

SLEEP DAY 6

Create a place to sleep.

For sleep today, I would like you to make sure that your sleeping environment is organized around you getting a good night's sleep.

De-cluttering the space around your bed, and the view from your bed, is a good way of keeping your sleeping space feeling peaceful and relaxing. You could spring clean your bedroom, or at least take away anything from your bedside table that is no longer needed. Like old magazines and books you have already read.

Open your bedroom windows at some point in the day to bring fresh air into your sleep space. Try not to take your laptop to bed with you, especially if it is to do work. Reserve your bed and the space around it for relaxing, winding down, and sleep.

When you sleep, your body rests and restores its energy levels. Undisturbed sleep is essential for ensuring you are getting all four stages of sleep. Sleep is an active state that affects both your physical and mental wellbeing.

If you live in a city or near an airport, or just have noisy neighbors, you could mask outside noise, which may disturb your ability to drift off to sleep peacefully, by listening to relaxing music or an audio book through headphones, taking them off just before you drop off to sleep. Getting a good night's sleep is one of the best ways to help you cope with stress. It also helps you create solutions to problems – you often wake up with a new perspective on a life situation after a good night's sleep.

NUTRITION DAY 6

Treat yourself today.

Plan, choose, and eat a special meal today, one where every bite tastes really great. The only proviso is that this meal should be packed with lots and lots of healthy energy and nutrients. I would like you to give thought to this meal, and take the time to focus on choosing the best ingredients that are available to you.

From now on, as much as possible, I would like you to avoid foods that don't add to your health. Try to avoid high-fat, high-sugar snacks, such as pastries, French fries, and chocolate bars, which are full of empty calories and contain very little nutritional value. You might not achieve a high level of healthy food every day, but try to focus on eating a well-balanced diet, choosing foods that naturally make you feel good.

Approximately 50 percent of your meal should be made up of fresh vegetables and salads. Visualize how your meal will look on your plate when you are planning your ingredients. Use as little processed food as possible, because it loses most of its fiber and a lot of its nutrients during processing.

Try to eat foods that are as close to the way nature created them. How about a piece of grilled fish with a jacket potato and a salad containing some raw chopped vegetables, or simply some lightly steamed vegetables? A vegetable-packed omelet or some lean unprocessed meat could replace the fish.

What you eat affects how you feel and if most of your diet is based on food in its natural state then the occasional chocolate bar or ready meal will not influence how you feel in the long term.

The key with everything is Balance. Do not abstain if you really desire something, as denying yourself often leads to overindulgence when your willpower eventually gives in.

If you eat something that you know is unhealthy, but you really fancy it or are in a situation where you don't have any choice, enjoy it and forget about it. I don't want you to feel guilty about eating anything. Guilt is a negative emotion that is likely to lead you to reach for less-nutritious comfort foods and not feeling fantastic.

Try to eat at least five servings of fruits and vegetables per day. It is a great starting point and provides your body with a good source of vitamins, minerals, and fiber, which will keep you feeling full and satisfied for many hours.

Eating the right foods can sometimes be hard to attain if you are not conscious of what you are eating. Take a relatively healthy diet, such as oatmeal for breakfast, a chicken salad sandwich on whole-wheat bread for lunch, and pasta with tomato sauce and a portion of broccoli for your evening meal. That is only two servings in one day. Consider adding a banana to your oatmeal and an apple mid-morning, and then have a chicken and avocado sandwich and add two types of vegetables to your evening meal – then you are up to your five-a-day already.

You could have a pure fruit smoothie instead of a chocolate bar in the afternoon if you need a boost of energy. The fruit sugar will satisfy the sweetness that we sometimes crave and it is also packed full of nutrients that will help you to feel fantastic.

ENVIRONMENT DAY 6

Feel the changes of energy in your different environments.

This could be noticing the change in temperature or humidity, or maybe how even the moon makes you feel at certain times. Or it could be at work, in meetings, in your car, on the train or subway, going to or from work, or perhaps at a sports game, or running in the fresh open air.

It doesn't matter whether the environment is pleasing or not, it is just about becoming aware of it and how it makes you feel.

Then I would like you to make a conscious move into a more conducive environment, even if it is later in the day. One that is more positive, uplifting, fresh, vibrant, and enjoyable, or get as close to one as you can.

This can be as simple as moving from one room to another, opening the windows, stepping outside into nature, going for a walk along the beach, or meeting up with a friend at a scenic place. The choices are endless.

Your environment makes a massive difference to how you feel. Getting into nature is the best place to connect with the environment – in the woods, by the ocean, up a hill or a mountain. This is due to there being more negative ions in the atmosphere in those areas.

Ions are atoms of energy that are either negative or positive. This is governed by the number of electrons versus protons there are in an atom.

Negative ions are tiny packets of electrical energy that bring vitality to living things. There are two types, large and small ones. It is the small ones that bring us more energy, and it is the Balance between the small and the large that affects how we feel.

The large, slow ions are more abundant in cities and polluted areas, and it is this abundance that makes cities energetically poorer.

Good luck. I hope you enjoy noticing the subtle changes in energy around you today. Noticing and feeling them is the first stage and, in time, you will be able to notice the change of energy in different environments, and also learn how not to be emotionally affected by them.

● ●

Actions for DAY 6

Day 6 brings the first Momentum element into the 9-day program.

- Achieve and Complete: Write a list of all the things you have yet to do in your life.

- Exercise: Do 20–30 minutes and set some personal goals.

- Personal Space: Feel and touch are the senses today.

- Sleep: Create a fresh and de-cluttered sleep environment.

- Nutrition: Choose and eat a special meal today – one that is healthy and tastes fantastic.

- Environment: Feel the change of energy in different environments today.

How are you likely to feel?

Moving into Day 6 can produce an energy shift. The Balance you have created over the last five days, together with the first Momentum element today, will start to create a higher vibrational state. Hopefully you can feel a spark of excitement about the endless possibilities that are within your grasp.

. . . .

'To dream is lovely; to dream and realize your dreams is fantastic.'

Today we are one step closer.

DAY 7

LEARN

Element 7 is LEARN, a Momentum element.

'Live from your heart through your mind.'

When we are children, we constantly learn and experience many new things each day. Learning new things creates Momentum and leads to growth.

Children have a natural thirst for knowledge because they are in a learning environment most of the time. They are seeing many things for the first time and are fascinated by the world around them. This is part of their natural development, and it makes them more open to new information and ideas.

Element 7 is about consciously learning something new each day, so that you can encourage freshness and Momentum into your life. For example, it might be learning something about a country you want to visit, or knowing more about a topic that interests you and have never explored. Our mind is a muscle and, like all of our muscles, it needs stimulation and a degree of stress in order to grow.

EXPANDING YOUR VIEWPOINT

Opening your mind to fresh ideas and information can help you to be free from habitual behavior, reducing any tendency for you to become fixed in your attitude and actions.

Being closed to new ideas slows down your growth, and causes you to stagnate and resist the natural Flow of life. Keep yourself stimulated by trying something new, or by building on the skills and experience you already have.

There are so many new and exciting things to do and learn, whether it is mentally, physically, or emotionally. Take some time to connect with yourself and learn how you truly feel and want to feel. What are you thirsty for?

Learning inspires us to think creatively, particularly if it is something that we are interested in. It stimulates and excites us. Taking action to learn encourages motivation, and motivation encourages more action.

You are already learning something new by reading this book, so why not continue and develop your Flow of learning? This is just the beginning – there is so much more to learn that will help you to grow.

Today I would like you to learn something new. Choose something that interests and intrigues you about a subject that you would like to know more about.

Did you know that Leonardo da Vinci invented scissors? I didn't, until today. Yes, this fact will not change your life, but it might make you think about how much potential one human being can have.

Learning something new can be thought-provoking. Learning something new and putting it into practice can be life changing.

What new thing could you learn and do today?

EXERCISE DAY 7

Do 20–30 minutes of exercise.

Connect with your body and mind today by learning a new sport like climbing, or challenge a friend to learn something new with you, such as salsa dancing, or karate. You will be moving your body and getting fit while having fun.

Another good reason to get your body moving today is to help your lymphatic system, which is responsible for your body's immunity. It removes harmful substances from your tissue fluid before it is returned to the blood and the rest of the body, and it relies on the movement of your body's muscles to pump this fluid.

So give your lymph system some help and go for it.

Post-exercise

An interesting and fun thing to do is to lie down immediately after vigorous exercise and notice what is happening inside your body. You will probably notice your breath first, as it is working hard to keep your body supplied with oxygen.

As this starts to calm down, you might be able to feel the energy inside your body buzzing and your muscle fibers twitching. You may even be able to feel your expanded energy field, now that you have increased its vibration.

A healthy body is born to move. Try adding a few minutes of stretching after exercising to keep your body strong and supple.

PERSONAL SPACE DAY 7

For personal space today, we concentrate on your sense of taste.

Your sense of taste is stronger if your mind can connect what you're eating with how it looks. Our sense of smell (and therefore taste) is strongest when we are hungry.

Today I would like you to focus on what you put into your mouth at one of your meals. Try chewing thoroughly and slowly, consciously becoming aware of how each mouthful smells and tastes. Did you know that a lot of energy is extracted from food while it is still in your mouth, before it is completely digested?

That is why, when you are tired, eating something restores your energy almost instantly, even before your food has actually been digested. Chewing properly releases more flavor and so extends the time that the taste of the food lingers in your mouth, because it spends more time in contact with your taste buds.

Therefore, by having awareness and taking more time to eat, you will develop your sense of taste and enjoyment, rather than having your thoughts somewhere else and not really noticing what you are doing. Being fully focused on what you are doing while you are eating will also help your digestion, and you will realize when you are full rather than mindlessly emptying your plate.

Learning to be present with your senses will bring awareness to whatever you are doing, helping you to become Balanced in your body and mind.

SLEEP DAY 7

Find a peaceful resting place.

Today I have a relaxing visualization and breathing technique for you to use just before you go to sleep. Make sure you have finished all your tasks for the day, so that you can get maximum benefit from this exercise before you go to sleep. You can also listen to the free audio download by visiting http://thewayjohnwhiteman.com/9-elements-audio/ and entering the password 'Feel Fantastic.'

EXERCISE: Preparing for peaceful sleep

Let's visualize a peaceful, restful place.

Close your eyes and imagine you are going on a calm and peaceful walk.

You could be strolling toward a beach, a wood, in the open countryside, or anywhere else that you find peaceful.

Feel the warm sun relaxing your muscles and enjoy how this peaceful place makes you feel.

There are 10 footsteps leading down to a natural quiet resting place. Start to walk down the steps. As you go down each step take a breath in and out, enjoying the beautiful surroundings around you.

Let's count down the 10 steps, breathing in and out with each step.

10... 9... 8... 7... 6... 5... 4... 3... 2... 1...

You reach a path that takes you to a comfortable, safe space for you to sit or lie down and relax.

You melt into this soft comfortable space and close your eyes, breathing in... and out... in... and out...

In your mind, imagine a beautiful blue cloudless sky.

If distracting thoughts come into your mind just let them turn into white wispy clouds, and allow them to pass across the sky and out of your mind. Bring your attention back to the wonderful blue sky.

It's now time to notice the sounds around you in your special place and to feel a gentle breeze on your warm skin.

It is time for you to leave your resting place now.

So walk back along the path again, toward the steps.

Walk up the steps, breathing in and out with each step upward that you take.

1... 2... 3... 4... 5... 6... 7... 8... 9... 10...

At the top of the steps you notice how relaxed and calm you feel, and it is now time for you to come out of this visualization.

Wriggle your fingers and toes.

Stretch.

And when you are ready, gently open your eyes.

Take a few moments to notice how relaxed your body feels.

Enjoy this relaxed feeling that you have created and have a wonderful night's sleep.

NUTRITION DAY 7

Today I would like you to practice mindful eating.

Mindful eating is all about eating consciously – being aware of the present moment and your appetite while you are eating. Are you really still hungry or are you already satisfied?

Mindful eating also involves learning to be conscious of the difference between hunger and other cues that can cause us to eat, such as painful emotions, boredom, tiredness, and habitual behavior. People often use food to fill a gap in their lives, such as loneliness.

Try to eat your meals in a calm environment where you can focus on what you are putting into your mouth, and whether you need to pause or stop eating entirely.

Take time to slow down, and make each meal an important and pleasurable part of your day. Get in touch with your body. Are your stomach and breathing relaxed?

Eating in front of the television or computer screen is commonplace, but it distracts you from realizing what and how much you are eating, as well as causing you to be in a less than ideal position and frame of mind to be eating.

Awareness of your hunger mechanism

A neural center in the brain called the appestat is the mechanism through which your body chemicals work together to signal feelings of hunger and fullness. It allows you to eat in response to hunger: in response to your body's needs.

Inactivity can cause your appestat not to work as well as it would in an active person. It can actually leave you feeling hungrier than someone who exercises, which is another great reason to exercise.

Other ways that we override our appestat are by eating high-fat and sugary foods. This is because you are taking in a lot of calories in a short space of time, which means you can take in more calories than your body needs before your appestat has a chance to tell you that you have eaten enough.

Also, if you eat too quickly, your appestat doesn't have enough time to register how much you have eaten, which causes you to eat a large amount before feeling full. You just start to rely on your stomach feeling uncomfortable, or your waistband feeling tight.

Being in touch with your body and mind by mindful eating is an easy way to stay healthy.

Today, I would like you to relish each bite, noticing the taste and texture of your food. Try putting your cutlery down between each bite and sipping some water. You could take a mid-meal break, have a chat for a couple of minutes, enjoy your companions and your surroundings, or get into the habit of taking a few deep breaths and thinking about what this food is doing for you.

Is it healthy and nutritious? Is it giving you what you need to feel fantastic?

Take small bites and chew them thoroughly. Become aware of what you are putting into your body and how it makes you feel.

Bon appetit.

ENVIRONMENT DAY 7

Keeping centered keeps your internal and external environments happy.

Notice how you react to the people in your close environment today. Try leaving a few seconds before you reply, so that you can bring freshness to how you respond to the people around you. This can stop you from responding with habitual reactions, so you are more connected and present with your interactions.

You might be surprised by the loving and wise replies that you create just by pausing and connecting with the situation fully. This will definitely generate a better environment for you, as it will affect how the other person responds to you, too. They will notice a change in you on a subtle level, because you are not matching their emotional vibration.

Often we can unconsciously mirror other people's energy and tone, which quickly affects how we feel and respond. It is our automatic defense mechanism (how we automatically react when we feel threatened), which has evolved over time, but does not always work well for every situation.

Replying from a more centered place in your mind, body, and spirit enables you to have awareness of the whole situation and works a lot better for you, leaving your energy and environment feeling happier, too. The Balancing elements can help you so much with this as, of course, they create the Balance needed. Over time you will find that you are more centered and calm when you do all five elements and less when you don't.

Connecting with your breath is one of the best exercises you can practice to help you stay centered. It is a good idea to practice breathing into your chest area and centering yourself at times when you are not being challenged first, so you get used to responding mindfully. Choose a couple of activities a day that you can do while focusing on being in your body.

When challenged, try to keep centered in your internal environment today. I am sure you will have lots of chances to practice.

PUTTING IT INTO PRACTICE

If someone knocks into you on public transport, or cuts you up when you are driving, make a conscious effort to stay centered and not to jump into thoughts about it in your head. Use any feeling of annoyance and anger to alert you to stay in your center. The negative emotions in your body come from the negative thoughts in your head about your situation. Staying centered helps you to view the actions of others just as they are: someone has bumped into you and that's it. It's not that they don't like you, think you are easy to push around, or don't respect you.

Stopping your mind from attaching negative thoughts and beliefs to a situation stops any negative emotions, and resistance to what is happening, growing in your body. Viewing them from a centered place in your body, not your mind, is the key to letting your negative emotions Flow. If you practice this it will change your life – it has mine.

If someone leaves the kitchen in a mess, don't react. Instead, accept the situation because resisting makes you feel horrible inside. I don't mean that you should let others take advantage. Just try to accept what is happening in the present moment without resistance, while staying connected to your body. Resolve the problem by asking or writing a note saying that you need the person's help to keep the kitchen tidy.

This is so much better than begrudgingly cleaning up, with your mind churning with negative emotions that make you feel hard done by, and so rob you of your fantastic positive energy.

'Let go of resistance and accept the present moment.'

You can apply this mantra hundreds of times a day. It will affect your relationships with the people in your life, and create a positive environment around you. This is a major lesson for anyone who tends to resist what is happening in their life, and it can have a massive affect on our energy levels.

RESISTANCE CREATES STAGNATION AND DEFENSIVENESS

Resistance to 'what is' creates lack of movement and stagnation in our bodies, and after a long period of time this can filter into the rest of our lives, leading to a resistance to any change.

Look back at your childhood and schooldays when change occurred all of the time and continual learning was taking place all of the time. Gradually, however, either because of different events in our lives, such as ambitions not being realized or facing problems, we progressively become more resistant to change and form beliefs about ourselves that aren't necessarily true. For example: 'I am stupid,' or 'I am a bad person,' and so on.

You can see how, if we don't learn to let things go and Flow with the situations we face in life, it is easy for resistance to form. It becomes a defense mechanism to life's ups and downs – causing us to put up barriers and react out of context to what is actually happening and, in so doing, not feeling wholly happy with our behavior.

Just reacting in the present moment from what is stored from our past history.

I call this our stuff!

We all have stuff that we carry around, things that have happened to us over the years. It is called life, and although it has brought us to where we are today, it doesn't have to define who we *are* today. It is much better to greet each new challenge with fresh eyes so we don't pre-judge and react to it with the perspective of past hurts. Like the earlier analogy of the river, life would be pretty boring if it didn't have the twists and turns that have created the characters we all are.

Noticing another person's defense mechanisms, and not reacting from yours, results in you both not talking to each other from your past hurts.

By now you will have made a connection to your internal environment and are beginning to see how not reacting to the present moment creates harmony in your external environment.

ACHIEVE AND COMPLETE DAY 7

Small, achievable goals create stepping-stones to amazing achievements.

Let's give some thought to living a life in which, at the end, you can turn to yourself and say: 'I did that. I am pleased I did that. I am proud I did that and I am happy I did that.'

Fill your life with special moments.

Yesterday you wrote a list of all the things you have yet to do in your life. I hope there were lots of exciting ideas on it, because today you are going to choose one and focus on doing it.

Choose one thing that you have not done and find out more about it. Choose something that is financially within your grasp and investigate prices or timings.

I remember the first time I wrote my list. I didn't have a lot of money, but I had on my list learning how to motor race, to watch a sunrise, and to play squash. As squash and the sunrise didn't cost very much, they were the ones I focused on first, while I started to save toward learning motor racing.

If you do this, you won't be the person who always wished they had done something. You will be the one with many brilliant stories and life experiences to tell.

Hopefully more than you can ever remember. How great is that?

Take one step at a time

My first goal was to play squash and the next was seeing the sunrise. I still remember the latter now. It was a frosty morning in late autumn, and we had to get up early in order to catch it as we had decided to bike to a great spot to make the most of this everyday event. We had to race to catch it and our hands were really cold from the morning air; we felt so alive and this simple event is still imprinted on my mind. Many months later I started to learn how to motor race. Many great things are achievable; it just takes a bit of focus and taking one step at a time.

I have helped a lot of people who have what I call medium-termitus. They have a great vision of what they want, but often fail to take the steps to get themselves there. It's like having a dream to run a marathon, but not doing the training to achieve it. What happens? Well, you never end up doing the marathon.

Having medium-termitus scatters your energy and keeps you from realizing your dreams. This can leave you feeling frustrated and disappointed, and sometimes lacking in self-worth, as you never seem to achieve any of your dreams.

So, as we did with Exercise on Day 1, we are going to start by taking one step forward to get some Momentum going.

Choose one thing from your list that can be achieved in the next month. Something that, within 30 days, you will be able to say, 'I did that, I did that... Wow, I did that.'

This will then spur you on to do the next exciting thing on your list.

• •

Actions for DAY 7

Today is about learning something new.

- Learn: Find out something new today.

- Exercise: Do 20–30 minutes today – try a new sport.

- Personal Space: Taste is the sense for today.

- Sleep: A relaxing visualization for you.

- Nutrition: Take time to consciously become aware of everything you eat and drink.

- Environment: Learn to react freshly to every situation you encounter.

- Achieve and Complete: Choose one thing on your list to learn more about.

How are you likely to feel now?

Today I am looking for you to be more thoughtful, and to start to become aware that how you feel and what you think are inextricably interlinked. You are now at the stage of working toward taking action, which will assist you in thinking less and feeling more.

This will then create more emotional Balance. You should be starting to have more awareness of how you feel and act, and feeling more of a spark of excitement about your life.

Igniting the spark within you and then taking little steps to get you either back on track and/or taking the steps to live your dream is, I feel, such an important thing to do in your life.

· ·

'Allow your light to shine as brightly as possible, as it will show you the way.'

SOCIAL CONNECTION

Element 8 is SOCIAL CONNECTION, a Momentum element.

'Create a life in motion, one where things come and go. When you allow yourself to let go more, and not to hold on to things too tightly, you create more space for you to receive.'

The energy of the people around you affects how you feel. The closer they are to you – whether in geographical distance or relationship – the more their energy will have an effect on you.

Choose whom you socialize with carefully. Notice the people who bring heaviness and those who bring lightness into your life. Some people can really drain your energy, either by their demands or their negativity. Being around someone who is hyperactive can also be draining. It is OK to be full of energy, which is what we are hoping to achieve with the 9 Elements, but it needs to be Balanced with focus and grounding.

People with too much Momentum and not enough Balance are likely to whip your energy up to their speed. At first, it can feel like they are exciting to be around, but when you part company you can often be left feeling exhausted.

Seek out interesting and fun people who are grounded and Balanced: people you really enjoy being around, have things in common with, and who stimulate you to open your mind to new ideas. If someone is dragging your energy down by being predominantly negative, just be aware and encourage them to change the subject to a more positive one. Talking about and being grateful for the great things we already have in our lives can sometimes change their mood.

On the other hand, being around positive people raises your vibration, and then you can pass this positive feeling and energy on to someone else, uplifting how they feel. It can be a smile or a compliment, something from the heart. Everybody is special and the energy of others affects how we feel.

We have the ability to make other people feel good and, although this is not the primary motivation in life, it so often repays us in beautiful ways.

It feels good to speak to people and ask them how they are. When you see someone else gain from your positive energy, it makes you feel even better.

Meet up with, or call, an uplifting friend today, and have a stimulating social connection.

EXERCISE DAY 8

Exercise to manage your emotions.

Today I would like to share a story with you about how exercise can help to manage anger.

Many years ago I used to get road rage. I would get into situations that, looking back now, seem really rather pointless but, at that time in my life, felt important. Have you experienced occasions when you are driving and become really annoyed with another driver? It is quite common.

Well, it seems unbelievable to me now, but I used to take things a little further than most, and often ended up in heated face-to-face exchanges. One day I got into an incident with a taxi driver. It was my fault, but my ego didn't necessarily see this at the time, and I ended up in a heated discussion with him.

He was massive, and for the first time I thought: 'Ouch, I am going to get crushed.'

Fortunately, my body remained intact, and I managed to talk my way out of it, but it dawned on me that if this continued, one day I was likely to get flattened.

My next thought was to learn how to look after myself, so that when I got into a situation, I would be able to sort out the problem physically. With hindsight, this was not the best idea I ever had, but I started taking karate lessons.

Now, the most amazing thing was that, in taking that physical exercise every day, my anger diminished, and as my anger diminished I found that, increasingly, didn't experience road rage.

I have used exercise countless times with my clients, and it works really well in overcoming anger and frustration. Exercise reduces the pressure of this energy and stops it from building up. Anger and frustration can be used positively to increase performance in some sports. See if you can feel the difference in how you feel both before and after exercise if, whenever you feel frustrated or angry, you channel this energy positively into exercise to push yourself that little bit more.

When you experience frustration or anger, any aerobic exercise will make you feel better, as it helps to burn off excess energy and tension.

There are certain types of exercise that are especially useful for this, such as boxing, martial arts, any high-impact exercise (where both feet leave the ground simultaneously), or anything that is extremely physical.

So today, just go and have fun: exercise, run, cycle, swim, dance, whatever makes you feel good and gets your body moving.

By now you will be able to gauge how much exercise, and the intensity of exercise, you need to feel good.

Let's release some tension and feel the positive effects that exercise brings.

Live life and enjoy each moment.

PERSONAL SPACE DAY 8

Practice breathing

Today, as you have done before, you are going to use your natural breath to help create some personal space. I would like you to inhale and exhale, while noticing where your breath goes, making sure not to force the breath at any time.

We are ideally looking for your breath to Flow to a point just below your navel. Once this is happening rhythmically, count the time in seconds that it takes to inhale and exhale. Look to match one with the other – for example, six counts in and six counts out. This creates a Balancing and calming effect within your body.

The following exercise will help you to breathe in a smooth, flowing rhythm with minimum effort. You can also listen to the free audio download for the exercise at http://thewayjohnwhiteman.com/9-elements-audio/. Just enter the password 'Feel Fantastic.'

EXERCISE: Using your natural breath

First, lie down on your back, with your legs hip-width apart, and place your arms by your side with your palms facing upward. Use cushions to make yourself comfortable. Gently close your eyes.

Step 1: abdominal breathing

Place your hands on your abdomen, with your middle fingers touching over your navel.

Observe your natural breath. You will notice that as you inhale your abdomen rises and as you exhale it falls. Just observe this for a few breaths.

Now begin to deepen, lengthen, and extend that movement. That is, while inhaling, let your abdomen rise to its limit and on exhalation let it fall completely.

Slower, deeper, more relaxed.

Keep your chest still during this entire process and only move your abdomen.

You will notice your fingers move apart as you inhale, and meet again as you exhale.

Continue this for five or six more breaths and then rest.

Step 2: thoracic (chest) breathing

Place your hands on the sides of your ribcage, fingers pointing inward.

Again, observe your usual breath, but this time focus your attention on your chest area.

You will notice your chest moving up slightly when you inhale and down when you exhale.

Again, observe this pattern for a few moments.

Now again, begin to deepen, lengthen, and extend this movement.

Slower, deeper, and more relaxed.

On inhalation, fill your lungs completely, feel your ribs lifting and expanding to the sides under your hands.

Then, as you exhale, let your lungs empty fully.

In this step, your abdomen is still, and only your chest is moving. Do this for five or six more breaths and then stop.

Step 3: the whole breath

This combines the above two steps.

Place your hands on your upper chest, fingers spread just below your collarbone. First inhale by filling your abdomen, and then CONTINUE inhaling as you expand and fill your chest.

Notice how your breath fills to the top of your chest and under your fingers.

Then exhale, first from your chest and, as it empties and falls, CONTINUE exhaling from your abdomen as it draws inward completely.

Gently engage your abdominal muscles to help fully empty your lungs.

This is one round of natural breath. Repeat this for five or six rounds and then stop.

Remember the pattern:

Inhaling – from the bottom to the top, abdomen then chest.

Exhaling – from the top to the bottom, chest then abdomen.

It is important to note that all of the above steps should be done WITHOUT strain. The natural tendency is to heave with effort. An easier way is to make it smooth and effortless. Go slowly and easy.

Initially, you might experience unevenness or bumps in this breathing process.

As with everything, with practice it will become more natural.

Over time, increase the rounds to 10, 15, then 20 and so on.

Picture your breath as a continuous wave-like pattern, as if it moves up from your navel to your throat with every inhalation and then down from your throat to your navel with each exhalation. It may take a few weeks of practice to perfect the ideal Balance:

A SMOOTH, flowing pattern with MINIMUM effort, and with MAXIMUM capacity.

And it is now time for you to come out of this exercise.

Wriggle your fingers and toes.

Stretch.

And when you are ready, gently open your eyes.

Take a few moments to notice how relaxed your body feels.

Have a wonderful day!

SLEEP DAY 8

For our sleep element today we are going to do a relaxing body scan.

I would like you to practice a 'body scan' before you go to sleep tonight.

The body scan is taken partly from the ancient practice of Yoga Nidra, which creates a state of conscious deep sleep and has been practiced for many years to create relaxation of the body and mind. Basically, it helps you to stop your mind from constantly thinking. When you try to subdue your mind, it can become restless, so by giving it something to focus on within yourself, rather than something external, it becomes one-pointed, which makes it less likely to wander off into random thought patterns.

How the body scan works

The change in focus of body awareness stimulates the different parts of your brain that control each and every body nerve. When you become aware of each part of your body, you are actually massaging the corresponding part in your brain as well. You establish the connection between your body and your mind. The impressions in your subconscious are brought to the surface and experienced, and then released as you focus on each part of your body. We use two main principles to do this: inner awareness and breath.

The body scan is an important exercise to experience, learn, and practice, even if you already fall asleep the second your head touches the pillow. By visiting http://thewayjohnwhiteman.com/9-elements-audio/ and entering the password 'Feel Fantastic,' you can access a free audio download for the exercise.

EXERCISE: Performing a body scan

This exercise is best practiced a couple of hours after you have eaten a meal and are in a warm semi-darkened room. You might need a blanket to keep you warm. Use pillows under your head and knees if you need support. Lie down, preferably flat on the floor or on a bed, with your legs outstretched and feet slightly apart, and your arms beside your body, palms facing upward. Now close your eyes. Try to remain awake throughout this body scan. It does take time to be able to stay awake and aware during the body scan because it is so relaxing, but you gain the most benefit if you can stay awake. Don't worry if your mind becomes distracted during the exercise, just bring it back to the present when you notice it drift off.

Take a few deep breaths and, as you breathe out, feel your cares and concerns flowing out of you, and your body relaxing.

Now become aware of your whole body lying there. Visualize your whole body lying down.

138

Feel your whole body lying down…

Feel the sensations of your whole body lying down, your whole body lying on the floor or the bed.

Now feel your breath, the rhythmic movement of your breath. Now become aware of your body and your breath.

Your body and your breath…

Now you are going to scan your body, focusing on all the parts of your body and relaxing each one in turn.

During this exercise it is helpful to see your body as an object, and your mind as the observer.

Repeat the part of your body in your mind, while bringing awareness to that part of your body.

Go to your right side:

Bring your awareness to your right-hand thumb, first finger, second finger, third finger, fourth finger, palm of your hand, back of your hand, wrist, lower right arm, elbow, upper arm, shoulder, armpit, side, waist, hip, thigh, kneecap, calf muscle, ankle, heel, sole, top of your foot, and your toes – one, two, three, four, five.

Go to your left side:

Bring your awareness to your left-hand thumb, first finger, second finger, third finger, fourth finger, palm of your hand, back of your hand, wrist, lower left arm, elbow, upper arm, shoulder, armpit, side, waist, hip, thigh, kneecap, calf muscle, ankle, heel, sole, top of your foot, and your toes – one, two, three, four, five.

Go to the back of your body:

Bring your awareness to the back of your head, neck, right shoulder blade, left shoulder blade, your spine, right buttock, left buttock, and your whole back.

Go to the front of your body:

Become aware of the top of your head, forehead, right eyebrow, left eyebrow, the space between your eyebrows, right eye, left eye, right ear, left ear, nose, lips, chin, jaw, throat, your right chest, your left chest, middle of your chest, navel, upper abdomen, and lower abdomen.

Now the major parts of your body:

Bring your awareness to your whole right leg, left leg, both legs together; your right arm, left arm, both arms together; the back of your body, the front of your body, your head, and your whole body.

Repeat to yourself, 'the whole body, visualize the whole body.'

Feel the awareness of your whole body. Feel your whole body lying down. See your body lying down.

Feel your body lying down and become aware of the meeting points between your body and the floor.

Your heels and the floor, your calves and the floor, your thighs and the floor, your buttocks and the floor, and your shoulder blades and the floor.

Feel all the meeting points of your body and the floor together...

Become aware of your natural breath. Feel the natural rhythm of your breath. For three breaths, feel your natural, spontaneous breath.

Now bring your awareness back to your body lying relaxed on the floor. Become aware of the room, the floor, the walls, the ceiling, and the noises in the room. Let your mind become completely external. Lie quietly until your mind is completely awake and externalized.

Now begin to start moving your fingers and toes slowly, stretching yourself and becoming aware of the room around you.

Once you are fully aware of yourself lying on the floor, slowly open your eyes. You have completed the body scan.

Take a few moments now to notice the benefits to how you feel.

Have a lovely night's sleep.

NUTRITION DAY 8

Today, keep your intake of refined foods and sugar as low as possible.

Eating whole-grain complex carbohydrates, combined with keeping your sugar intake low, will give you a steady stream of energy. This will stop you feeling hungry soon too, and prevent you from reaching for a calorie-dense snack to give you an energy boost.

Eating foods that are high in sugar and refined carbohydrates, such as white flour, can cause your blood sugar level to rise rapidly. This is because large amounts of sugar are quickly released into your bloodstream, causing a rapid rise in blood sugar that triggers an exaggerated release of the hormone insulin to lower it.

Your lowered blood sugar causes you to crave something sweet again, or a caffeinated drink to give you an energy boost. This pattern of yo-yoing blood sugar piles on the pounds and can leave you feeling drained and listless.

If you skip or delay a meal, this also causes your blood sugar level to lower, and you may become irritable, angry, and weak. You are also more likely to reach for a high-sugar snack as a quick fix.

So, for lots of sustainable energy:

- Eat three meals a day containing fresh fruits, vegetables, and whole-grain carbohydrates (these are slower-release carbohydrates, such as oats, brown rice, whole-wheat bread, and pasta.)

- Have a healthy snack of nuts and seeds in preference to fast-release carbohydrates (sweet, baked, or fried foods) mid-morning and afternoon.

- Stay hydrated.

You will be getting the amino acids, vitamins, and minerals that your body needs. In addition, the slow-release carbohydrates will help you to feel more Balanced, have lots of energy, and feel fantastic.

It is quite easy to eat a 500-calorie pastry and still feel hungry. But if you eat 400 calories of whole-wheat pasta and vegetables, you will have energy for several hours and won't feel the need to reach for a high-sugar energy boost.

Balance is the key. No extremes, just a healthy, balanced diet, as close as possible to being as nature provided.

ENVIRONMENT DAY 8

Look around to find out how your environment affects how you feel.

It can be a good idea to take five minutes of personal space before you come into any new environment. For example, at the end of a working day, try stopping on your journey home, preferably in a place where you can be close to nature, so you can let go of the stresses of a busy day. It could be as simple as parking a short distance away from home, taking some deep breaths, listening to some relaxing music, or, even better, taking a short stroll in a natural setting. This will help you make the transition from your work environment to your home environment.

If you work at home, the two environments can merge, so it is important not to let a stressful work environment spill into your home life (and vice versa). At the end of the day, switch off your computer and phone, and change your environment by going for a walk before 'coming home' again.

It will create awareness of how you are feeling, and give you a chance to let go of your work pressures, clearing your head and helping you to become centered in your mind, body, and spirit.

Going straight home after work can lead you to walk into your house feeling stressed-out and, maybe, reacting to the people around you in a way that you might regret later. Or perhaps you will be unaware of how your words and actions are affecting your partner, children, or other family members. In turn, this affects their energy and starts a cycle of negative energy. This can be avoided if you are aware of how you are feeling in each moment, and then actively look to improve your state of mind. If you feel good, then it helps everyone around you to feel good, too.

So, try giving yourself five minutes to connect with how you are feeling, and to let go of any negative feelings. Now you are centered and ready for the different pleasures and demands of your home life, particularly if your home environment is very challenging.

SEEK OUT POSITIVE ENVIRONMENTS

Have you been in a Balancing environment today? Did you have a chance to get out into nature, and how did you react to the people around you?

Achieving a positive internal environment will enhance your external environment and bring Balance to your whole life. The opposite is also true, but the optimum is to have both.

The energy of the natural environment can have a big influence on our energy and how we feel. If you can become aware and connect with this natural energy, and learn to Flow with it, you will become more in Flow with life. Notice the seasonal energy around you. Notice the energy of the Earth and its energy on a macrocosmic level with the whole of nature and the microcosmic level of your body.

In recent decades, as the modern world has developed, we have become more detached from the natural world. Cultural and other changes have caused us to lose our connection with nature, as we have moved into a more scientific way of looking at the world from the outside–in, which means we tend to overlook our natural, intuitive inside–out intelligence; we have become desensitized to nature. Many wonderful new inventions have been made, but many of us have lost the very essence of humankind.

Our urban way of living has disconnected us from nature. Children who are brought up in cities, or who spend little time in a natural environment, find it difficult to associate with the natural world because it has become less of a part of the society in which they live.

CONNECTING TO THE NATURAL WORLD

The seasons affect how we feel because we are intrinsically connected to them on a deep level. The energy of spring, for example, influences us because we, too, are part of the natural world and feel the effects of nature as it starts to gather energy. As the season gains Momentum, we see and feel this energy literally bursting out all around us, causing tiny buds to appear on trees seemingly overnight.

Spring is a great time for us to get in tune with this energy, and we often instinctively mirror it in our lives. People often start new projects, feel compelled to spring clean their homes, or learn something new. They feel spurred on to take action by this energy – 'they spring into action' and 'the sap rises.' Take some time to connect yourself with your environment and become aware, and Flow with, the energy of the beautiful season you are in.

The action for this element today is to become in tune with this seasonal energy in a natural environment.

ACHIEVE AND COMPLETE DAY 8

Today I would like you to set a date for completing one of your dreams, and commit to that date.

Now you have a list of all the things you would like to do in your life, and have chosen to focus on doing one of them, the next stage is actually doing it. Today I would like you to set a date and commit to achieving it.

It is so easy to put hurdles in your way, so I would like you to commit to a fixed time when you plan to Achieve and Complete one of your many dreams. After you have successfully completed one, enjoy the feeling that you get from the Momentum and then move on to the next one. But today I would like you to commit to the first one.

One great way to do this, if appropriate, is to do whatever is on your list with someone else. It is fantastic to climb a mountain, but even better to experience doing it with someone else. You then have a shared experience that creates a special moment. Maybe your partner would like to do this with you, or perhaps a friend, or just someone you know. It is not essential but, when you have someone else there to encourage and support you, it helps you to stay committed and focused.

So I would like you to put down this book for a moment and set a time for when you are going to do it, and then take whatever steps are needed to book it, or start it. NOW, just do it, go on. You will feel really good once you have achieved one of your dreams.

What you do today will affect what you do and how you feel tomorrow *and for the rest of your life.*

LEARN DAY 8

Learn something new today.

What talents do you have stored up inside that you haven't yet released? Don't let your age put you off learning something new. We all have different ways of learning, and maybe you have not yet accessed all your abilities, or had a chance to unfold your talents. Sometimes we hold ourselves back through fear of failure, but it is much better to try and experience, than never to pop your head out from inside your shell. Don't keep your talents locked up inside. Express yourself.

Learn about something that really interests you, something that fills you with excitement, and gives you new inspiration for life. Learn experientially, learn intuitively, and put yourself in the environment to learn; break new ground and become relaxed in your new environment.

Learning by experiencing

There is a big difference between learning by reading about something and learning by actually doing something. For example, reading about how to play tennis and actually physically learning to play is very different. Learning by experience creates a knowing inside you; it becomes part of your physical make-up rather than just an idea, a belief about something. A belief can be strong, but knowing is unquestionable. So, if you really want to know about something, experience it.

• •

Actions for DAY 8

Social Connection is the new element for today.

- Social Connection: Notice people with positive and negative energy.

- Exercise: If you feel frustrated or angry, use exercise to release pent-up energy, stress, and tension.

- Personal Space: Connect with your natural breath.

- Sleep: A relaxing body scan to quieten your mind and put you in the mood for sleep.

- Nutrition: Keep your intake of refined foods and sugar low today.

- Environment: Get into nature and become in tune with the season's energy.

- Achieve and Complete: Book and commit to achieving one of your dreams.

- Learn: Learn and experience something that fills you with excitement.

How are you likely to feel?

By Day 8 things will be beginning to Flow. I would like you to take a few moments to remember how you were feeling on Day 1 and how you feel now.

You have come a long way in such a short space of time. You will be noticing which elements you need more or less of in a day depending on your mood, and becoming aware of how your moods and feelings are changing all the time.

These moods and feelings are yours and no one else's. No one makes you feel a certain way, because it is impossible for this to happen. You create moods and feelings. And it's up to you whether you choose to react and engage your mind and emotions with them or not.

. . . .

Below are the results of a test that I created to help people see how much Momentum or Balance they have, and which of the 9 Elements they need in order to enhance their lives. This test has revealed some interesting statistics so far on how the 9 Elements improve how people feel, and their levels of happiness. The results are based on a survey of 3,230 people.

1. Exercising three or more days a week (Element 1):

   Fantastic 16.14%

   Good 42.28%

   OK 23.39%

   Not great 14.64%

   Rubbish 3.55%

2. Having personal space on most days, as well as exercise (Elements 1 and 2):

   Fantastic 20%

   Good 49.19%

   OK 19.33%

   Not great 9.42%

   Rubbish 2.06%

3. Sleeping well, having personal space, and exercising (Elements 1, 2, and 3):

   Fantastic 24.74%

   Good 55.13%

   OK 15.55%

   Not great 3.88%

   Rubbish 0.7%

4. Eating fruits and vegetables most days, as well as sleeping well, having personal space, and exercising (Elements 1, 2, 3, and 4):

   Fantastic 27.57%

   Good 54.2%

   OK 14.49%

Not great 3.28%

Rubbish 0.46%

5. Being in a positive environment most days, as well as eating fruits and vegetables most days, sleeping well, having personal space, and exercising (Elements 1, 2, 3, 4, and 5):

Fantastic 29.83%

Good 56.9%

OK 9.94%

Not great 2.76%

Rubbish 0.55%

6. Living their dreams most of the time, as well as being in a positive environment most days, eating fruits and vegetables most days, sleeping well, having personal space, and exercising (Elements 1, 2, 3, 4, 5, and 6):

Fantastic 35.11%

Good 58.03%

OK 4.58%

Not great 1.52%

Rubbish 0.76%

7. Consciously learning something new three times a week or more, and living their dreams most of the time. Along with being in a positive environment most days, eating fruits and vegetables most days, sleeping well, having personal space, and exercising (Elements 1, 2, 3, 4, 5, 6, and 7):

Fantastic 39.28%

Good 54.46%

OK 3.59%

Not great 1.78%

Rubbish 0.89%

8. Spending quality time with friends and family three times a week or more. Consciously learning something new three times a week or more, and living their dreams most of the time. Along with being in a positive environment on most days, eating fruits and vegetables on most days, sleeping well, having personal space, and exercising (Elements 1, 2, 3, 4, 5, 6, 7, and 8):

Fantastic 42.22%

Good 52.22%

OK 3.34%

Not great 2.22%

Rubbish 0%

And this leaves just one day to go. The results for Day 9 will be shown later.

Enjoy your day.

DAY 9

BEING PRESENT

Element 9 is BEING PRESENT, and brings
all the other elements together.

*'There is only the
present moment.'*

Well done, you have now started to experience the effects of bringing most of the 9 Elements of The Way into your life. Your energy will be Flowing really well now, and you will have started to create some Balance and Momentum in your life. You may already be sensing that you can live the life you have always dreamed of, one in which you are full of energy and feel fantastic.

REVIEWING THE LAST EIGHT DAYS

Let's have a brief look at what we have been focusing on over the last eight days.

For the first five days you learned the five Balancing elements, which are Exercise, Personal Space, Sleep, Nutrition, and Environment. These elements help you to become Balanced in your mind, body, and spirit, giving your mind the space it needs for more inspired actions.

Then, for the last three days, we have focused on the three Momentum elements, which are Achieve and Complete, Learn, and Social Connection. These elements help you to live your life to the full, using the energy you have created for taking action.

In addition, all of the elements have been working on boosting your energy vibration from the inside–out; from your inner core, outward into the world in which you live, helping you to feel better and attract higher vibrational energy into your external life.

This leaves just one more element to introduce and, in my opinion, I have left the best until last. This element alone has the potential to have a massive effect on your life, and it encapsulates all of the other eight elements.

Put simply, Element 9 is where children live most of the time, but as we grow older we become more focused in our minds and this wakefulness often slips away.

Being present means living in the present moment as it unfolds, with moment-to-moment awareness. Why is this so important? Well, being present gets you to focus your energy and allows you to connect with what is happening right NOW.

We often rush through what we are doing, *looking* and *striving* to get to a better moment, even if we are enjoying the present moment that we are living. If we slow down and truly experience what is happening right now, we will find that what we are seeking is contained within the present moment already.

Whether we notice this consciously or not, we all do it, and it can lead to living unsatisfied lives, forever searching and seldom stopping to be present. Our minds are often full of thoughts about what has happened to us in the past, or about what we are going to do in the future. Whenever you are able to become present in your life, it becomes so much richer, because you are fully present with what you are doing. You begin to see the detail rather than just the surface layer of everything.

Being present is so important because there is only the present moment: this is where we are all the time, everything else is either past memories or imaginings of the future.

WHAT HAPPENS WHEN WE ARE NOT BEING PRESENT?

To make sense of why it is so important, let's take a look at what happens when we are not present.

Our mind is somewhere else. That's it! A part of us is somewhere else. We are not fully present in our life. We live life through a veil, clouding our experience of what is happening now.

Sometimes a startling event can catch us and bring us into the present moment, such as a beautiful sunset, a full moon, or a rainbow. I vividly remember once seeing a whale lift its tail out of the water, bringing me immediately into the present moment. A rare sight in nature, such as this, awakens all of your senses to that moment, and the image is clearly imprinted in your mind.

All these special things have the ability to stop your train of thought and bring you into the present.

If we could learn to focus our attention in the present moment I believe we could enjoy more vivid lives, ones where we see the beauty in every moment. This type of present awareness creates the special moments that make up our lives. How many special moments do we miss every day because our minds are somewhere else?

WHAT ARE WE MISSING?

It is amazing what beauty we miss when we are not fully present in our lives.

The sun on our face as we step out the door, or the fresh morning air meeting our breath. The smile on someone's face or the sparkle in their eyes.

These are the things we miss because our minds are already thinking about our journey ahead. This frequently happens with the people we love; often, we are only partially listening to them while thinking about something else left to do, or constructing our reply before they have even finished speaking. We are so conditioned to *doing* that we miss the full experience of *being* with them.

WHY ARE WE NOT FULLY PRESENT IN OUR LIVES?

We are not fully present with what we are doing for a variety of reasons. We live in a fast-paced world, which means we are always thinking of the next thing we *need*, or think we *need*, to do. So, while doing one thing we are almost always somewhere else, our minds caught up in thinking about what we will do next instead of what we are doing now. In The Way we call this 'rushing.'

When we are not rushing, we are usually seeking something to fill our minds, so that we can get a break from the chatter of our minds. Or, we fill our time doing something because we are not used to being present with ourselves.

> *'Just doing nothing... don't even*
> *try to do nothing... just being.'*

You might say, 'Well, I am present, I am aware of what I am doing already.' But for most people, most of the time, their mind is either in the past or in the future, and therefore very rarely fully present. It is not until you start practicing this awareness that you realize how often a part of your mind is almost always somewhere else. Buddhists call this present moment awareness 'mindfulness.'

LEARNING TO BECOME PRESENT IN OUR LIVES

My preferred way to teach myself new things is by taking one small step at a time, and then by repetitively practicing or layering until each new thing becomes grooved inside me.

Once practiced and experienced, a belief becomes knowing. You have already experienced being present, as it has been weaved into the last eight days, in the exercises and into all of the elements. This has gradually helped you to become more and more present, and more and more connected to how you feel without consciously thinking about it.

Being present plugs you into life and, because your mind is not consumed with repetitive thoughts, space is created for inspired thoughts to rise, generating Momentum in your everyday life.

DON'T SEE THOUGHTS AS BEING BAD

I don't want you to view all thoughts as being negative, because once you are Balanced in mind, body, and spirit you will find that repetitive negative thought patterns will lose their energy and fade.

A thought can only exist if we pay attention to it. Being present makes you conscious of some conditioned beliefs that are perhaps not serving you anymore, or never did. Things we have repeatedly heard or labeled ourselves, without really questioning their truth. We all have them, as they have been passed down to us, usually inadvertently, by our parents, teachers, and society, and by our mind-based assumptions of how we think things are.

'We are the ocean, and our thoughts are the waves. Just watch the waves and enjoy being the ocean.'

WORRY AND ANXIETY DON'T EXIST IN THE PRESENT MOMENT

I feel the most important aspect of being present is that it eliminates worry and anxiety. The only exception is when you are actually experiencing a present moment crisis. Even then, present moment awareness helps you to keep calm and see the bigger picture, bringing calmness and clarity to the situation. Your mind is brought into focus on the reality of what is happening in the moment, and not worrying about what might happen later or tomorrow.

Worry and anxiety don't have a place in the present moment. They are your imagined thoughts. When you are thinking these thoughts, your mind is focused on what might happen, rather than what is really happening. It is speculation and your body is reacting as if it is real. Once viewed with present moment awareness, the thoughts are clearly seen as imaginary ideas, not reality.

IMAGINED THOUGHTS

How many times have you worried about something only to find that, in the end, the situation you were worrying about doesn't happen or, if it does, it isn't half as bad as your mind had imagined it would be?

Take a little time to remember this if you are one of the many people who experience anxiety. It's easily forgotten when the mind has become grooved in this way of thinking. Worry and anxiety are created purely by the mind, not reality, and they don't actually exist in the present time. In focusing mostly on your mind you lose the Balance between your mind, body, and spirit.

'Contentment and happiness are found in the Present Moment, Balanced in the whole of you: your mind, body, and spirit.'

BALANCE AND MOMENTUM IN THE PRESENT MOMENT

For a moment, imagine a car on your drive. Perfectly balanced and pristine in every way. Engine tuned, wheels perfectly balanced, and with a full tank. This car is perfectly Balanced in every way, but if it doesn't get driven it will lack Momentum and not go anywhere.

Now imagine a car without this Balance. Out of control, racing down the road, steering wheel wobbling, and debris flying off everywhere. This is the perfect example of over-Momentum. You might be getting somewhere fast, but it is a very bumpy and uncomfortable ride.

Lastly, imagine you are in the ultimate car. It has Balance and it has Momentum. (This is the car that you

have been preparing for yourself to become from Day 1.)
As the driver of this car, however, your mind is focused
down the road and round the bend, and instead of enjoying
your fabulous well-tuned car, you miss everything.

You miss the present, you miss your surroundings, you
miss the possibility of a new route, you miss the smiles of
the people you are with, and you miss life.

By bringing Element 9, Being Present, into your
everyday life you feel the Balance, you feel the Momentum,
and you feel fully connected to life and your journey in
every way possible.

LEARNING HOW TO BECOME PRESENT

We apply being present to all of the elements today. You
may have found that this has been gradually happening
over the last eight days, as connecting with your senses
and being aware of your energy spontaneously brings you
into the present moment.

What does Being Present feel like?

Being present is the element that encapsulates all of the
other elements. If you can bring this quality into all of
them, it really plugs you in and switches you on to your
life, creating a different quality of experience. It is as if
a thin veil has been lifted, and everything looks clearer,
sharper, and more vibrant – as if you are seeing things
for the very first time. You feel much more in tune with

the world around you and, on a practical level, everything feels and becomes easier to do.

You will begin to experience moments of not thinking, which can be quite surprising and enjoyable. Being present brings you relief from the noise of mind chatter and the repetitive thoughts circulating in your head, as well as creating space for something fresh to come in.

Registering special moments

Being present means recognizing what is happening in any given moment, allowing you to be wholly part of it. Awareness of the present moment is being fully switched on to how you feel and what you are doing. It brings you out of your head and into the whole of you: your mind, body, and spirit. In the following elements today we will learn ways to enhance this present moment connection.

You can use your breath, your senses, and being in a stimulating environment to bring yourself into the present moment. For example, watching a sunset or playing in a great football or tennis game brings you into the present. You know the feeling when you are fully engaged in what you are observing or doing. Try watching or listening to something with your whole body; listen as if your whole body is one big ear.

Once you learn to live in the present moment it stops mind chatter from taking control of your life. It keeps you in touch with life right now, and not your past or projected future. Be awake to the present moment, feel alive, live life to the full. Do all of the things you have wanted to do with your life. When you live life to its fullest extent, you are spontaneously brought into living in the present moment.

Today, I would like you to register a special moment that happens to you during the course of your day. It could be, and often is, something that doesn't cost anything – a smile from someone, watching leaves blow in the wind, or hearing a bird singing. It could also be an achievement at work, or learning something new. I would like you to experience it fully today, with your whole mind, body, and spirit.

EXERCISE DAY 9

Be with what you are doing and your doing becomes being.

When you exercise today, I would like you to focus on your senses. Take everything in – your environment, how the ground feels under your feet, the detail that you can see in things, the sounds around you, and the sound your breath makes while you are exercising. Feel and connect with your body as it moves, keeping your full attention on yourself as you are exercising.

To stop your mind from wandering you can say to yourself: 'My attention is with my body exercising.'

And then run through your senses:

I can feel my feet on the ground, I can hear my breath, I can smell grass in the air, I can hear birdsong, I am connected with the whole of me – my body, mind, and spirit – while exercising.

This exercise will help you to stop your mind from slipping into past and future thoughts. Just try it. It might sound a bit silly, but you will notice how good it feels to be truly with your body while you are exercising. Your mind might wander, but this is OK, just acknowledge it without judgment, and bring your focus back to yourself in the present moment.

The positive effects of exercise

By now you will definitely be noticing a difference in how you feel. You should have more energy, and be less stressed. Exercise produces a relaxation response that relieves many stress disorders and creates a positive interruption from your day-to-day worries. As well as the health benefits, aesthetically it only takes a couple of weeks of consistent exercise for you to start to feel your clothes fitting differently, and see that your muscle tone has improved. Pound for pound, muscle burns more calories at rest than body fat. So the more muscle you have, the higher your resting metabolic rate will be (that's the rate at which your body burns calories.)

Have a great exercise day; the sky's the limit now. Fantastic!

PERSONAL SPACE

Create some breathing space today.

Focusing on your senses brings you into the present moment. Today I am giving you an exercise to connect you with your breath. When you do this exercise, you instantly become present with the core of you, your very being.

Personal space is all about being at one with yourself, fully in the present moment. For at least five minutes a day, just take time to be, instead of constantly doing, or thinking about what you should be doing. This brings a freshness to how you move forward into a doing moment.

Today I would like you to notice where you are breathing to in your body. Then, after a few breaths, focus your attention on breathing into the area about an inch below your navel, allowing your abdomen to rise with the in-breath, and fall with the out-breath for about five minutes.

Just focus on your breath coming in and going out: deeply, slowly, quietly, and rhythmically, without straining or overfilling your lungs at any time.

Connecting with your breath in this way at various times during the day will allow you to become present, de-stress, and bring vitality and energy into your body. You will also start to become aware of areas where you are holding tension. This awareness will then start to become part of your everyday life, giving you the opportunity to relax, let go, and just be.

Connecting to your breath, your senses, or nature for five minutes a day will help you to become fully alert and in the present moment. This will have the effect of stopping your mind from racing ahead into the future, or going over past events. It creates breathing space to sense how you are feeling internally in the present moment. It brings clarity, so that you will be able to respond instead of react to the external world around you throughout the rest of your day.

Enjoy the space it brings.

SLEEP DAY 9

Be present.

For sleep I would like you to be present with everything you are doing during your wind-down routine this evening. Be with all of your senses and take a little extra time to really connect and care for yourself, as you gradually relax your body and mind before going to bed.

I would also like you not to drink any alcohol today. This is because when people drink alcohol they start to disconnect from being in the present moment. With the bigger purpose of feeling fantastic I would like you to stay connected and present.

People often get into the habit of using alcohol to help them relax in the evening, to switch off after a busy day, and to help them sleep. This is quite understandable, as it quickly disconnects you from your busy mind, but it comes with the price of losing your connection to your conscious mind.

Alcohol intake can easily become a habit, especially if it is being used to cover up issues that would be better faced with clarity so a solution can be found. Problems like overworking, depression, or an unfulfilling life, etc. It is not about judging: I am not saying that people shouldn't drink. We all experience life differently and many people have various reasons for wanting to disconnect from their lives. Awareness and moderation consciously allow you to observe habits and take action to change aspects of your life that enhance and don't detract from life's vibrancy.

Alcohol can affect some people by worsening their anxiety and worry. They become less conscious; their minds become numb and, because they are no longer present, their mind chatter takes over. In some people the energy becomes heavier and heavier, causing depression and even anger, which can burst out in a harmful way.

In order to help you feel fantastic, we are aiming to work with the natural rhythm of your body so you don't need to take stimulants and relaxants to make yourself feel better. We want you to boost how you feel naturally, without the cycle of highs and lows that caffeine, alcohol, or other drugs can create.

It is best to manage how you feel by boosting your energy naturally, so your vibration gets higher and higher. Rather than disconnecting from your conscious mind, becoming present is a more natural way to wind down. When you are present you are more conscious of your mind chatter, able to see your thoughts more clearly, and not allow them to consume and become you.

Solutions to problems can only be found in the present moment. Solutions create clarity and space to see the bigger picture. Covering them up just delays you living the life you love to live.

We are looking for you to give yourself the best opportunity to have a thoroughly restful night of sleep. This will be achieved by allowing your mind and body to wind down, relax and rest, and recharge naturally. When we give our bodies a rest from alcohol we usually wake up with a clearer head, feeling healthier and more refreshed.

NUTRITION DAY 9

Be mindful of your food.

As before, notice where your food originates from, and be mindful of how your body feels while you are eating it. Become aware of how different foods make you feel. Some people may be sensitive to certain foods, such as wheat or dairy products, which can make them feel tired, experience bloating, or lead to skin conditions such as eczema. Being present while you are eating will help you to notice the different effects food can have on your energy, and connect any physical symptoms to the foods that are causing them.

CONSCIOUS EATING

Today I would like you to be present with your food, and to develop a habit of conscious eating. Take your time to focus on the following:

- Be in the moment while preparing and cooking your meal.

- Connect all of your senses with the food you are eating.

- Look at what you are eating and engage fully with it.

- Notice the noise it makes in your mouth.

- Smell and taste every bite.

- Notice how this food is making you feel, and how it is affecting your energy.

Being present while preparing and cooking your food can turn a 'means-to-an end' chore into something truly enjoyable. Really be with your senses, feel the textures of the vegetables as you pick them up, enjoy the sensation of the water on your hands as you wash them, feel the warmth of the handle of the peeling knife in your hand, and the floor beneath your feet. Be mindful as you move around the kitchen, and fully engage in every element of the task. If your mind drifts off just bring your focus back to what you are doing.

In my experience being present brings a different quality to this everyday task; it really connects you with your food, and so mindful eating occurs naturally because you have already really connected to what you are about to eat and are in the present moment.

ENVIRONMENT DAY 9

Being Present helps you to see the bigger picture.

I would like you to bring all of your senses together in the environment today. Become aware of the energy around you. Focus on placing yourself in a positive energy environment as much as you can.

If a situation occurs in your day that you view as negative, see it as 'just the way it is.' If someone around you is grumpy, see it as just where they are today and don't allow their energy to affect you. It only becomes yours if you choose to take it onboard, and into your energy.

Soften, and see things in a lighter way and try to view the events of the day from a broader perspective. If you can remember to be present when someone is irritating you, you can keep calm, take a few breaths and stay connected. You can have compassion for what is happening in their life, but you do not have to become energetically involved. With present moment awareness you can see the bigger picture and won't get caught up in their drama.

Mind chatter is at its strongest when we think life isn't going how we think it should. The repetitive negative dialogue that goes on in our minds after someone has said something that upsets us, just leads to further pain as we turn it over and over in our heads. If you can catch yourself and just stop paying attention to those thoughts, they will drop away easily. You will have to really want to feel better, or they will become your focus and lower your energy.

ACHIEVE AND COMPLETE DAY 9

Create focus

Being present really comes together with this element, Achieve and Complete, when you are doing one of the things from your list of things that you have always wanted to do. This is because in doing that special thing, you naturally come into the present moment because you really want to fully experience it.

Focus the power of your attention and intention on what you want to do. Being fully present while you are doing a task helps you to keep focused on one thing at a time and stops you from scattering your energy on many tasks at once, which causes you to feel unsatisfied, distracted, and unproductive.

Be in the present moment and bring yourself into Flow with what you want to get done today. Prioritize the most important task that needs doing that will feel great in your life. Sometimes you might find that this isn't what you have been doing, as you have been putting other things in your way, and this has been holding you back.

We can choose to climb a mountain with rocks on our back and find every step hard or we can choose to put down the rocks and experience an easier, lighter journey with the amazing views that surround our every moment.

You will find that as each task is completed you create Momentum, which in turn sets up the energy you need for the next one. If awareness is lost, however, the doing can easily turn into over-Momentum, causing you to lose Flow and start rushing.

LEARN DAY 9

When you learn something new today give some thought to expansion.

What could you do with this newly learned information? Could you create something? Maybe pass the knowledge on to someone else? Use it to develop yourself or your work further?

Learning new things gives your life Momentum. Don't push and strive, though, just let the learning Flow. When your learning is in Flow you will be able to feel it – it will feel effortless and create Momentum.

What can you learn on a larger scale today that will take you further forward on the journey of your life?

Stay present and learn who you really are

Where did your current beliefs come from? Are they still true for you today? To answer deep questions and contemplate your life requires present moment awareness, so you can search for your truth within. Being present helps you to feel it with the whole of your body, rather than just using your mind.

Take a few moments today to become present with the essence of who you are at the core of your being. Connect with your heart and learn who you really are beyond the labels that have formed inside you over the years. Many people feel they have lost their true selves, and it takes a little time and awareness to learn who they are and reconnect with how they want to be in their lives.

SOCIAL CONNECTION DAY 9

Be Present.

Being present with the people around you brings a beautiful quality to your interactions. You find that your connection with your partner is so much richer than just passing time. The person you are with feels you are really there for them, and you get a real sense of who they are beyond the surface layers of their personality.

If your mind is somewhere else and the other person notices, perhaps only on a subtle level, something is lost from your time together. You miss the full connection that might have brought about something special – maybe a common interest, a shared dream, or a great story.

Part of being present includes being an active participant in your relationships. Humans have a need to connect with one another, but with such hectic lives many of us find ourselves doing so in a perfunctory way. For example, when you sit down to speak with someone, do you give them your full attention, or are you sending a text message, composing your answers, or thinking about what you need to do later at the same time as listening to them?

Have a great social connection. Truly be with the other person and listen to them with your whole body. We are often caught up in our heads and used to acting from conditioned responses, which causes us to not really be there with our friends and family. Your interaction is a little stale, as your mind is often somewhere else. When you start a new relationship, however, you are usually fully present with the person you have just met because you are very keen to get to know them. You often hang on to their every word and study their reactions to yours.

When you are fully present with a person, you often start to see them in a new light. You become more aware of their energy, you notice the sparkle in their eyes as they retell a story from earlier that day, and you remember why you love them so much. You are connecting to who they really are, the very essence of their being.

Think about a connection that you've had today or yesterday. Were you truly with the person or people in front of you? Or were you caught up in your thoughts and point of view, missing out on engaging with them on a more satisfying and exciting level? It is not about trying hard to listen to them, it is about truly being with them. Giving them the space and time to express what they want to say. You will find that you learn a lot more about them because you will hear what they are saying from a higher level and with an expanded awareness. Your essence will start to communicate with their essence. This is the body's natural intelligence, or intuition, which is a lot wiser than our minds alone.

Sometimes, understandably, you may feel resistance against certain people and not want to be fully present with them, especially if it is someone who you find irritating, or who pushes your buttons. But listening to them with your whole body will enable you to see the bigger picture of their life. You will be able to create the space that is needed for you not to react, or build resistance within your body to what they are saying. Listening with your whole body will help your emotions to come from a calmer space, as our emotions and feelings come from our mind-based thoughts, beliefs, and values, which can often lack the broader view.

THE END OF DAY 9

That is the end of Day 9. Wow, well done, you have completed it! I must say it has been quite a journey for us both. The next stage is to put the 9 Elements to use in your daily life, and you'll find some tools on pages 221–238 to help you to make full use of them and keep your energy raised.

How are you likely to feel?

Day 9 has brought in the element of the Present Moment. Becoming aware of where you are Now. Switching off your mind by simply letting go, and not holding on to things with your mind.

Being present will minimize worry, anxiety, and fear. You will still experience these feelings at times. We all do. It's part of life's richness. You know now, however, how to manage these emotions – by thinking less, not more.

The 9 Days have taken you on a journey that will have created more Balance and Momentum while experiencing Present Moment awareness. On Day 8 we looked at the results of doing Elements 1 to 8. Element 9, Being Present, changes the results dramatically.

By practicing all of the 9 Elements people felt:

    Fantastic 72.23%

    Good 27.77%

• •

Element 9 brings all of the other elements together. Each element in isolation isn't really enough to create happiness from the inside-out, but just bringing in a few every day can make a marked difference to how you feel and how you feel is how you live your life.

So to summarize, how you feel is really down to you – you have all of the tools now. On the days you don't manage to do all of the elements, awareness of which ones are missing is all you need, so you can take little steps to bring them into your life over the next few days.

I don't manage to do all of the elements every day. What I do though is make sure they are the priority in my life, because feeling fantastic is important to me.

In just 9 days you have come such a long way. I have so much respect for people who follow this program. I hope you are very proud of your achievements, too, and I sincerely hope you are feeling fantastic.

PART III
The Way Forward

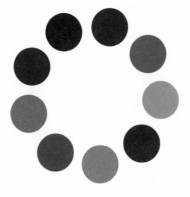

*'You have the power within you
to be and feel fantastic.'*

9 ELEMENTS PRESCRIPTION

We all are blessed with a full set of emotions and feelings. We all feel joy, happiness, love, pride, depression, anxiety, and anger to name a few. It is, however, worth becoming aware of how strongly we feel these emotions, and which ones we experience to a greater degree in each and every day.

Awareness of how to manage how you feel is valuable. I am looking for you to experience emotional Flow. All this requires is for you to not hold on to any emotional state, whether it is good or bad, as this would be going against 'what is' the natural Flow of life, unfolding moment by moment.

When you are in Flow everything is just right, just as it is. You are not resisting the present moment, so even the feelings that are labeled bad are manageable because there is no resistance. Everything is viewed and felt from a centered place of peace within you.

Holding on to emotions traps this energy inside you and keeps you in resistance mode, building tension and bringing you out of the present moment and Flow. This leads to a cycle of mind-based worry, anxiety, and fear.

The 9 Elements will help you to stay connected to what is real and what is mind based. By using them you will begin to notice whether you need more Momentum or more Balance to stay in Flow.

MANAGING YOUR EMOTIONS

Let's have a look at a few common situations, feelings, and emotions and show you, in general terms, how certain elements could be used in order to bring an improved emotional state to your mind and body. Emotions and feelings are complex and do intertwine, so please see these as general recommendations. If you have any symptoms that are not improved when you incorporate the 9 Elements into your life, I suggest a discussion with a medical practitioner would be appropriate.

Genetics do play a part in how you feel, but in my experience with many clients, only a minor part. You have the power and ability to self-manage how you feel, and with awareness, the ability to understand that sometimes your feeling is there for a good reason.

Sometimes you will notice a time delay. For instance if you haven't slept well, this can take a couple of days before it begins to show up in your emotions as irritability, or the feeling of not being able to cope. If you haven't exercised for a good few days, then this can start to appear as stagnation, frustration, or anger. Our emotions come from our thoughts, beliefs, and values, which are based in our minds. The common approach is to analyze the mind, but this keeps you in your mind and stimulates this mental activity even more. The 9 Elements creates less mind thinking and more active experiencing, which Balances your mind, body, and spirit. Our negative emotions are an indication that we are out of Balance.

FINDING SOLUTIONS

Below is a list of the most common problems that people face, and which elements can be used to make you feel better, so you can help yourself to create happiness from the inside–out. This guide is based on my personal experiences, and I hope you find that, by looking up your symptoms, you'll also gain more awareness of the causes and find the solutions.

Mind Chatter

Symptoms

Your head is filled with constant mental noise: repetitive thoughts and unconscious ramblings that are strung together and have little benefit to where you are now. Now is the only place you will ever be! For much of the time these thoughts are negative and hold you back from enjoying life to its fullest extent.

Causes

Stress, worry, not being present, living in our heads, rushing, and over-Momentum. We are mind, body, and spirit. Mind chatter is an over-stimulation of the mind, which, unless rebalanced, can sometimes trip out. Once aware, you can take steps to restore your mind, body, spirit Balance, and calm this over-stimulation naturally.

Solutions

Increase your Personal Space (Element 2), as this will give you clarity and connect you more to your body. Look to increase positive activities that uplift and inspire you. Take time out to 'be,' and immerse yourself in the present moment.

- Slow down the Momentum in your life, as this will help you to become more effective.

- Learn to stay centered in your body and become present with the whole of You in every moment.

- Notice where your breath goes to in your body and set aside more time to stop and just be in your day.

- Avoid caffeine and food or drinks with sugar or additives.

- Practice yoga, running, and meditation: being in a natural environment, as well as connecting to nature, will balance your energy.

Increase the five Balancing elements of The Way. Practice being present, along with reducing the three Momentum-based elements.

'Just "be," less "do".'

Depression

Symptoms

Prolonged, mild, or deep feelings of hopelessness and misery, and an inability to find any joy in life.

Causes

I have found that depression comes progressively on two levels: depression created by lack of Momentum, and depression created by lack of Balance and Momentum. The latter is a much deeper form and needs more effort to lift your energy out of this negative spiral.

Solutions

In my studies, mild depression is due to lack of Momentum. Generally, this form of depression is brought about by lack of achievement or direction, or simply by being stuck in a rut. I am sure virtually all of us have experienced feelings of heaviness, either in the course of a typical day, or over a longer period of time.

Succumbing to mild depression and taking early action, even if this action is just to become aware of these feelings, is paramount. Achieve and Complete (Element 6) and Social Connection (Element 8) can rapidly lift a heavy feeling and bring the lightness and excitement back into your life.

Left unnoticed, or without action, mild depression can slip into deeper depression. This often occurs when someone with mild depression doesn't manage to do and maintain the five Balancing elements.

Exercise (Element 1) is especially important here as it kick-starts your energy into feeling good. The other four Balancing elements – Personal Space, Sleep, Nutrition, and Environment – all have their parts to play in improving your energy vibration and creating a route out of depression.

Depression goes hand-in-hand with repetitive, often negative, thought patterns, which pull you away from being present, and cause anxiety, worry, and a downward spiral of your energy, leaving you with a feeling of helplessness.

If you are in this sliding situation, take immediate action by introducing the Balancing elements back into your life. These nurturing elements will give you the lift you need, helping to stabilize your situation, and bringing back the vitality that has become overshadowed by the dominance of your mind.

Worry and Anxiety

Symptoms

Worry: being troubled with negative thoughts and images about real or imagined problems that your mind is attempting to avoid. You may experience shallow breathing, tension, and insomnia.

Anxiety: nervous confusion marked by excessive uneasiness and apprehension, typically combined with compulsive behavior, and, in some cases, panic attacks. You may also experience heart palpitations, muscle weakness, shallow breathing, and irritability, and have trouble concentrating.

Causes

Anxiety and worry occur when your thoughts are not focused in the present moment. You might be living in the moment in your body, but your mind is somewhere else. Progressively, you become disconnected from what is happening now, missing out on much of the joy and vibrancy that the present moment brings.

Many people experience these mind-based conditions because they are not Balanced in their mind, body, and spirit – they are living predominantly in their heads. Bringing yourself into the present moment stops your mind from picking up and running with these thoughts. Worry and anxiety only exist in the past or the future, not the present.

Solutions

Being Present (Element 9) and Personal Space (Element 2) can help people overcome worry and anxiety. These emotions can become habitual, so the first stage is to learn to become more present in your day-to-day life. If you have had worry and anxiety for some time, though, you might find that you habitually slip back into not being present. Layered learning becomes very effective in this case. In other words, practice being present until it becomes layered and grooved.

Connecting with your senses brings you into the present moment and helps you to be more Balanced in the whole of you, your mind, body, and spirit. Take five minutes of Personal Space to notice where you are breathing to in your body; if it is your upper chest, practice dropping your natural breath into the area just below your navel. Do this several times a day, or whenever you start to worry or feel anxious.

Try focusing on the solution rather than the problem, as this will immediately make your situation feel lighter, and help you to start taking steps to resolve it.

Practice watching your thoughts, but don't pick them up, just watch them. A thought can only persist if you give it your attention. You don't have to stop the thoughts, just rest in your body and witness them coming and going.

Fear

Symptoms

An unpleasant emotion caused by the threat of danger, pain, or harm.

Causes

In my experience there are two different types of fear: shock and mind-based fear.

Shock equals actual fear that is occurring in the present moment. For example, caused by shock, such as after having a car accident.

Mind-based fear equals imagined fear that is coming from the mind. Fear is a continuous extension of worry. Worry leads to anxiety and develops into fear.

Solutions

Shock fear can only be reduced when you change your Environment (Element 5.) Mind–based fear is calmed by moving into the present moment and, increasingly, practicing the five Balancing elements. Shock fear is relatively rare – 99 percent of fear is mind based and brought about by not being in the present moment.

Although fear is generally irrational, the perception of danger feels very real. A person experiencing a panic attack will often feel as if he or she is about to die or pass out. Connection with the breath increases oxygen flow and connects the person with their body. If they can watch the fear they can see it is separate from them. I had a client say that she wasn't present enough to do that, as her mind was too fearful. I replied that she was very present. Who was watching her mind be fearful?

When you have feelings of apprehension or dread, you feel jumpy or anticipate the worst. A solution is to move toward the problem. When you face fear you are moving into the present moment and the feelings of fear fall away.

Frustration

Symptoms

Being upset or annoyed as a result of being unable to change or achieve something.

Causes

Generally, frustration is caused by things not going the way you think they should. You often feel that other people create frustration, but no one can make you feel a certain way – only you can choose to do this. Other people might be a trigger, but it is always your choice whether to embrace these feelings or put them down.

Solutions

Everyone feels frustration at times. Left in your body to build up, the pressure can result in outbursts of anger.

Exercise (Element 1) is the simplest and easiest way to reduce and eliminate frustration. It will return Balance to your mind, body, and spirit, and bring clarity to your day. When you have clarity you enjoy life more, and it allows you to perform to your optimum.

Frustration can be viewed as similar to a pressure cooker. Personally I find that frustration begins to occur in me if I don't exercise for a period of three days. The feeling inside me begins to feel heavy; I become less motivated, less vibrant, and more reactive than proactive.

Just by noticing this feeling growing inside you can give you the awareness you need to take action. Look to remain Balanced in the body and present as much as possible. When you are present you are able to see a situation with clarity, and take positive action while remaining calm.

If exercise is not possible in that moment, and you feel frustrated, look to the other Balancing elements to help reduce this pressure. In particular, change your Environment (Element 5) because this creates the Personal Space (Element 2) to bring more Balance into your system. This is an effective solution to frustration, provided you spend your Personal Space time connecting with your breath and body, rather than staying in your head churning around your thoughts about the situation.

Anger

Symptoms

Strong, rigid feelings of annoyance, displeasure, or hostility that often feel as if they are uncontrollable. They can be accompanied by a feeling of heat rising in the body.

Causes

A build up of frustration inside your body fueled by negative thoughts over a period of time. If not released, it can rapidly display itself as anger. Quick-moving expressions of anger, coupled with awareness, allow your body to let off steam and stop it from building up. Or anger can be positively focused into a sport like cycling to enhance performance. However, anger often isn't managed or witnessed and Balanced, causing a person to verbally or physically attack another person.

Solutions

All the Balancing elements and being present can help you witness your anger and the situation. Regular exercise, in particular, restores Balance by enabling you to let off steam. Martial arts or boxing are aerobic exercises that can help considerably.

Lack of Self-worth

Symptoms

Lacking confidence and self-respect. Lacking belief in yourself and your abilities.

Causes

A lack of self-worth is generally created over a long period of time. Once again, it can be self-created or conditioned into the way you feel by external influences.

People who lack self-worth have generally lost direction a little and find they are not connected to, or feel able to live, their dreams.

Solutions

Lack of self-worth often goes hand-in-hand with mind chatter and is often a response to repetitive external environmental influences that lower your energy and self-esteem.

To improve your self-belief, create a strong focus by incorporating the five Balancing elements (Exercise, Personal Space, Sleep, Nutrition, and Environment) into your life, as a first step, and then create forward motion from Balance by introducing the Momentum elements.

Momentum is often in people with low self-esteem or a lack of self-worth. Sometimes it is just that they are on a different path from the one their heart desires. By creating more Balance, you allow inspired thought to ignite your passion for life once more. Following your dreams and focusing on Achieve and Complete (Element 6) will get you living your dreams.

Without internal Balance, Momentum can be short-lived, hence the need to create a Balanced foundation before embarking on increasing Momentum in your life.

Loss

Symptoms

Deep sadness and yearning caused by parting from or losing something or someone you really care about.

Causes

Loss usually results in a lack of Momentum and depression.

Solutions

Allow yourself the time you need to come to terms with your loss, and then, very gradually, begin to take progressive action to increase more Momentum into your life until your confidence builds up enough to take bigger steps.

See yourself as a child again, learning to walk. Take it slowly and focus on creating a secure environment to help support you. This might be your family home or with friends.

Loss can leave a person with a lack of Momentum for a long period of time. It can also do the opposite and create a singular focus in someone because they shut down their feelings and their senses, and battle through their loss instead of grieving. Grieving allows your emotions to Flow.

Flow (enlightenment) is the intention in all of my teachings. Allow yourself to feel and show your emotions – fluidity is key to feeling good. Realize, however, that there is a time when the lack of Momentum and void, which is created by loss, needs to be filled again. And the best way to fill this void is by bringing in positive and life-enhancing Momentum.

Stress

Symptoms

A state of mental or emotional strain or tension, usually as a result of adverse or demanding circumstances.

Causes

Similar to frustration, stress is a build up of pressure and tension that is either externally or internally imposed on you. But, whereas frustration generally stays inside your head, stress impacts your mind and your body, creating tension in your muscles. Over-stress is where the demands on you exceed the amount you are able to give. Over-Momentum causes stress, as you have very little Balance and you tend to do far more than your body and mind can cope with.

Solutions

Everyone needs a certain amount of stress to promote growth, so when stress is operating within a small band it can be seen as positive. Being able to manage your personal stress is more an art than a science, as everyone has a different stress tolerance level to different things.

Having too much stress can cause an emotional breakdown. Panic attacks, migraines, and similar stress-induced conditions are managed best by increasing your awareness of Being Present (Element 9), together with action to maintain Balance in life by focusing on the five Balancing elements (Exercise, Personal Space, Sleep, Nutrition, and Environment.) If you already live with great Balance in your life and still experience stress, then reduce your Momentum to improve your overall Balance.

Alcohol Abuse

Symptoms

Addiction to the consumption of alcoholic drink; alcohol dependency.

Causes

There are a variety of reasons why a person might over-consume alcohol. Some of the most common reasons are depression, over-stress, lack of self-belief, and pain avoidance. Or it could be purely through having an addictive need, or a social connection in which a lot of alcohol is routinely consumed.

Solutions

Always look for the reason or cause rather than treating the symptoms. If you consume alcohol, when do you consume it? Do you use drink to disconnect from life, to switch off stress, or to manage depression? Have you become, or are you becoming, habitually addicted? There is a big difference between having a social drink and having a drink out of need. If there is a need that causes you to crave alcohol, look to manage the need.

Answers can be found by noticing which elements you are missing out regularly, as well as becoming aware of your overall equilibrium between Balance and Momentum. Alcohol switches off the present moment and shuts down your brain – like pulling a plug out of the wall. Become more, not less, connected to life by managing 'need.'

Obsessive-compulsive Disorder (OCD)

Symptoms

An anxiety disorder caused by having thoughts that produce uneasiness, fear, and worry, and resulting in repetitive behaviors.

Causes

Characteristically, OCD is a mind-based disorder brought on by not being present.

Solutions

Balance yourself in your body by using breathing exercises (Element 2) and Being Present (Element 9), which will calm your mind and help you to reduce this obsessive habit. The more you think about something the more it is likely to happen. Practicing the 9 Elements will help you manage your thoughts and your emotions.

Bipolar Disorder

Symptoms

Manic and depressive emotional swings, or manic ones only.

Causes

The direct cause of this disorder hasn't been scientifically established, but the triggers that create these emotional swings are typically an excess or lack of something: an imbalance that causes the swing to happen. Caffeine, medication, hormones, or alcohol can cause this swing of instability to occur.

In our fast-paced society, Bipolar Disorder is increasing dramatically. It is usually brought about by a lack of being present, over-Momentum, and not enough Balance.

Solutions

Balance and awareness can bring stability to the mood swings associated with Bipolar Disorder, and reduce their impact on a person's life.

Concentrating on the Balancing elements (Elements 1–5) is the first step, followed by reducing Momentum and learning to be more present in every day. The excitement and rush of Momentum is addictive, enhancing and increasing the possibility of bipolar episodes. With awareness you can bring more Balance into this aspect of your life to stop it getting out of control.

Lethargy

Symptoms

A lack of energy and enthusiasm; a feeling of drowsiness and tiredness in which everything appears as being hard work and heavy.

Causes

Lethargy can be created by poor dietary choices, not drinking enough water, sleeping too much, lack of exercise, or as recovery from a period of over-stress or over-Momentum.

Solutions

Feeling flat and lacking in energy happens to all of us at times. A long period of lethargy, however, creates depression. It is perfectly normal sometimes not to rely solely on sleep as your moment of down time, to stop, and get bored once in a while during the day allows you to stop and reflect on things.

If, however, you feel lethargic over a prolonged period of time, what you are likely to find is that you are lacking in many of the 9 Elements. Getting going again and creating the stimulation does take a little effort, but you will notice the improvements immediately and feel amazing. To begin with, look at where you are in respect of the Balancing elements – in particular, Nutrition (Element 4) – and then focus on the other Balancing elements to restore more Balance in your life. This will return your internal energy to a more comfortable place before you embark on Momentum-based activities.

Over-Momentum

Symptoms

Rushing around, continuous mind chatter, not enough time in the day to get everything done, too much stress, shallow breathing, and lack of personal space or downtime, which leads to burnout or illness.

Causes

Awareness of over-Momentum occurs when you find you are rushing from one thing to the next, have endless lists and are always saying that you have no time. There can be many reasons for this state. One is over-giving to other people and not listening to your body when it is tired or overworked; another is an inability to prioritize, because there is little clarity. There is also taking on too much as a way of shutting down emotions that relate to past hurts; not creating any time for yourself; guilt; or just pushing yourself too much.

Solutions

People who experience over-Momentum just don't stop. When they do stop, they are generally exhausted. Increasing internal Balance reduces over-Momentum because it brings about clarity, which then alerts the person to the need for a priority on creating personal space and more personal time.

Someone with over-Momentum doesn't usually want to slow down, as the feeling is addictive. This is why prioritizing the Balancing elements is important. If someone with over-Momentum increases the Balance in their life, they automatically feel better and are able to be more effective in what they are trying to accomplish. As a consequence, life becomes easier, stress is reduced, health is improved, and happiness increases.

Lack of Momentum

Symptoms

Boredom, lethargy, unhappiness, a lack of direction or fulfillment, and no direction or passion in life. People with a lack of Momentum can resort to alcohol abuse and disconnection, and are more likely to experience depression.

Causes

Someone with a lack of Momentum can be somewhat isolated and without good social connection. Lack of Momentum can occur through getting knocks or setbacks, things not going to plan, or unfulfilled dreams

Solutions

Connecting with a person with a lack of Momentum to stimulate their passion and desires again is a great way to create more Momentum. A person with a lack of Momentum is more likely to slip into depression at times, and this is why keeping both Balance and Momentum in your life is essential.

Connection with the Momentum elements, especially Achieve and Complete (Element 6), is where someone with a lack of Momentum should focus. When you are connected to living your dreams, and have a passion for life, everything begins to happen. You feel lighter, more motivated, excited, and expressive. This is because you are back on course and moving into Flow.

Guilt

Symptoms

A heavy feeling of having done something wrong, or failed an obligation or commitment.

Causes

Guilt can arise when the self-imposed expectations of yourself or others are not met.

Solutions

Guilt is a mind-based sensation that can be reduced by being more present and increasing body awareness. When you experience guilt you are in your mind, and not Balanced in your body or your spirit enough. In letting go of thoughts by having moment-by-moment present awareness, and maintaining a good Balance (Elements 1 to 5), you quieten your mind into accepting 'what is,' and then taking action in the present moment to get life back on track. By letting go and going more with the Flow, you will find that guilt is just an aspect in life that holds you back from connecting with the whole of you.

Regret

Symptoms

Feelings of sadness or disappointment.

Causes

Regret occurs when you think you should have done something, but failed to do so.

Solutions

As with guilt, regret is purely in your mind and the solution is to become more present in every moment. Where you are today isn't where you will be tomorrow or where you were yesterday. By taking small, positive steps today, in the moment, tomorrow can be anywhere that you set your intention to go.

Lack of Motivation

Symptoms

Lack of desire or willingness to do something; lack of enthusiasm.

Causes

Lack of motivation occurs when you have lost your desire or passion to do something, perhaps because of an unexpected setback.

Solutions

Motivation comes *from* action and not *before*. Motivation is an internal energy feeling you get once your energy is moving. Momentum *creates* motivation. So the solution to becoming more motivated is to move toward doing something. As with anxiety, when you move toward a worry, the worry goes away – the same is true for motivation. The biggest question relating to motivation relates to finding your purpose and maintaining motivation to do things that have positive effects on your health and wellbeing.

Lack of Clarity

Symptoms

Lacking the ability to communicate with yourself and others clearly.

Causes

Lack of clarity can come through a lack of understanding about a situation, or, specifically in this context, a fuzzy feeling in your head that often goes hand in hand with lack of sleep, personal space, and present moment awareness.

Solutions

A combination of two of the Balancing elements – Personal Space (Element 2) and Sleep (Element 3) – together with increasing present moment awareness, can help with restoring enough Balance to become clear in your mind about things. Without quality in these areas your emotional Balance becomes unstable. By taking the time to put these elements to the forefront of your day, it will allow you to re-establish more Balance and, in turn, restore your clarity.

Divorce

Symptoms

A separation between a couple, which can create stress, anxiety, fear, depression, lack of self-worth, lack of direction, guilt, regret, anger, resentment, and other emotional outbursts.

Causes

Usually your partner ☺.

Solutions

A divorce is usually an unsettling and, potentially, devastating period for one or both partners. It can unearth many negative feelings and emotions, including anger, resentment, and lack of self-worth. Focusing on the Balancing elements creates a counter-Balance to the stressed and strained emotions during the process.

In energy terms, there are similarities to a river splitting into two separate rivers. At the point at which the river divides, there is turmoil. If you can accept that this is the way of divorce, this awareness will help you realize it is the Momentum in your life that is being affected by the loss of this close connection. While maintaining focus on the Balancing elements, give more time to use the Momentum elements, in particular Achieve and Complete (Element 6), to prevent yourself from becoming lost in a tide of emotions. If you stay where you are, the churning effect of divorce can make you feel as if you are in a tumble dryer. By keeping Balance and Momentum in your life to help create and realize your dreams and aspirations, you will gradually Flow to calmer waters.

Being Bullied

Symptoms

Stress and anxiety, feeling worn down and often getting ill, with increased sensitivity to even the smallest of issues, which can lead to a lack of self-worth or self-belief.

Causes

Bullying usually occurs over a sustained period of time. It can start with constant nit-picking and criticism, or being singled out and belittled. Or by being embarrassed in front of others or manipulated in ways that are unkind or thoughtless.

Solutions

When you are being bullied, in energy terms you shrink into hiding within a shell. Consistent bullying can leave you fearful and bring about a lack of self-worth and self-esteem. Being bullied tends to create a lack of Momentum in you.

Momentum allows your dreams and aspirations to flower, which in turn improves self-worth and self-esteem. Always approach an increase in Momentum with

Balance. When you have Balance in your life you become more centered, so the bullying will take less of a personal toll. In particular, focus on Environment and Achieve and Complete (Elements 5 and 6) to reduce its effects and allow your energy to grow stronger. Whenever possible, do not enter the environment where bullying occurs, and only do so when you are feeling centered and Balanced.

Element 6 can reignite the spark inside you to raise your energy to such a level that it doesn't matter how other people act toward you. A bully always looks for weakness. When you show that you have no weakness and your energy is strong, you will find that the issue with a bully is with them and not you. It is never about you.

'See yourself as a light and
allow yourself to shine.'

THE END AND THE BEGINNING

Now you have had a chance to experience the 9 Elements and have started to feel the benefits of Balance and Momentum, the way forward for you now is to bring them into your everyday life. I have included some useful tools at the end of the book to help you chart your progress.

You have a 9 Elements Daily Checklist on pages 223–226, where you can tick off the Elements you have completed each day over the next few weeks. It's good to have an overview of which Elements you are consistently including or missing out each day or week.

You could make your own version of this chart on your computer, print it out, and place it somewhere prominent as a visual reminder to take five minutes of Personal Space or to eat a nutritious lunch and move your body. This could be placed on your fridge, your desk at work, on the inside of a kitchen cupboard, or in your diary.

It can take a few days for the effects to take place as they are gradually changing the Flow of your energy, but some of the elements, like Exercise or Personal Space, can make you feel better instantly. These elements are valuable natural tools that can easily be added into your life. And now you have the tools to raise your vibration, you will notice when it drops and do something about it. You will no longer be lost in your emotions and tossed around the river. You have the ability to steer yourself back to a calmer, happier life.

You can use the different exercises over and over again to help you stay in Balance with your mind, body, and spirit. Especially when your mind chatter keeps you focused in your head, and out of the present moment.

BARRIERS

Do any of the 9 Elements create feelings of resistance in you?

Sit and observe these feelings for a moment. Don't judge yourself, just observe them without any resistance. Don't let your mind start to run a dialogue with these feelings. Keep your awareness of them in your body for a few moments and be with the emotions that arise. Create a moment in stillness; this alert observation can reveal some very insightful thought patterns. Try asking yourself: are these thoughts true?

Stay with your body and your heart will show you

the truth of whether this is an old, unconscious thought pattern. Keeping in your body, and not your mind, with this inquiry will help you to break down these barriers.

With clarity, you will hear the thoughts as soon as they surface and be able to dismiss them straight away.

FEELING GUILTY

Some people feel guilty about spending time on themselves.

Don't feel guilty about doing something for yourself. Does feeling guilty make any sense to you? Did you choose this belief, or have you just accepted it unconsciously? I don't think anyone would expect you to suffer in the name of love or duty. Spend some time doing the things you love to do, and see how your happiness radiates outward and lifts others.

TRIGGER POINT

Use any discordant feelings as a trigger for using the 9 Elements. Use the checklist and see which ones you have been missing out. It helps you to notice if you start reverting back to an 'OK' way of life, rather than feeling fantastic and living life to the full.

Use the *memory* of how you feel after doing each element, instead of your mind. Our minds like to think up excuses, often telling us why we shouldn't do a certain element. For instance: I have no time, I'm too tired, it's boring, or whatever your mind-based sense of self throws at you.

When this happens, just notice that you are not *solely* your mind, as something that is *not* your mind is able to watch these thoughts and has a choice as to whether to pick them up or not.

STAYING MOTIVATED

The motivation will come from feeling better. That's why it is important for you to *do* and not just *read* this book. Once you have felt the benefits of experiencing the 9 Elements, you will have the 'knowing,' not just the theory, that you possess the tools to make yourself feel better, whenever you need them.

It is preferable to use the 9 Elements every day, but they are always there for you to use whenever you start to feel emotionally challenged, or wish to feel happier and more connected to life.

Once practiced, the 9 Elements become second nature, allowing you to self-regulate how you feel. The motivation comes from the *doing* and not *before the doing*.

Doing the 9 Elements on a regular basis, and putting how you feel as a top priority in your life, means that your motivation will show itself as you get back in Flow with your journey.

MAKE HOW YOU FEEL A PRIORITY

If you really want to feel better and enjoy a life that flows easily, but find that you drift back to habitual behavior that keeps you from living your dreams, please don't be hard on yourself. This is just the way that your old behavior has become grooved. A new way forward is to really commit to living a happier life, and create a moment of intention to choose a different path. Make it your priority; connect with your desires in the way you did at the very beginning of this book again and again. Then, with your desires as your main focus, commit to doing the 9-day program perhaps three times a year. Mark the dates down in your diary. Make how you feel a priority three times a year. This new way of thinking and behaving will then carve grooves on this new path.

Each time you follow the 9-day program you will absorb a little bit more of the information and experience deeper positive effects, giving you more opportunities to bring happiness into your life from the inside–out. For some people, things have to get pretty bad before they take action, and that's OK, too. There really is no judgment here, just the willingness for you to find a life that brings you joy.

FIND YOURSELF AGAIN

I don't think you have to change in order to live an enlightened life. I think that in the process of letting go of what you are not, the true You comes shining through. So, don't be afraid to shine.

THE WAY

The Way is a philosophy of life that has developed and evolved over many years and many situations. In this book you have been introduced to the 9 Elements that form the foundation of The Way.

The Way is the bigger picture of life. It brings in a Balance of mind, body, and spirit to help you to live a centered life, full of awareness and happiness. The teachings, although simple, are deep-rooted, and truth and energy play important parts in living a life in Flow.

The Way is coming...

So we reach the end of our time in this book. It would be lovely to hear how you get on. My thoughts are with you.

Thank you and take care,

John x

'Every ending is a new beginning.'

9 DAYS AT A GLANCE

Use the checklist below to chart your progress, and to make sure you are bringing all of the 9 Elements into your day. You could make your own version of this chart on your computer, print it out, and place it somewhere prominent as a reminder to take 5 minutes of Personal Space, or to eat a nutritious lunch and move your body. This could be placed on your fridge, your desk at work, on the inside of a kitchen cupboard, or in your diary.

	1	2	3	4	5	6	7
1. EXERCISE							
2. PERSONAL SPACE							
3. SLEEP							
4. NUTRITION							
5. ENVIRONMENT							
6. ACHIEVE							
7. LEARN							
8. SOCIAL CONNECTION							
9. BEING PRESENT							

9 ELEMENTS DAILY CHECKLIST

This checklist is a little reminder of which Elements you should be doing, according to which of the 9 days you are on. You could use it to tick them once you have you completed them each day.

DAY 1

- Exercise

DAY 2

- Exercise
- Personal Space

DAY 3

- Exercise
- Personal Space
- Sleep

DAY 4

- Exercise
- Personal Space
- Sleep
- Nutrition

DAY 5

- Exercise
- Personal Space
- Sleep
- Nutrition
- Environment

DAY 6

- Exercise
- Personal Space
- Sleep
- Nutrition
- Environment
- Achieve and Complete

DAY 7

- Exercise

- Personal Space

- Sleep

- Nutrition

- Environment

- Achieve and Complete

- Learn

DAY 8

- Exercise

- Personal Space

- Sleep

- Nutrition

- Environment

- Achieve and Complete

- Learn

- Social Connection

DAY 9

- Exercise

- Personal Space

- Sleep

- Nutrition

- Environment

- Achieve and Complete

- Learn

- Social Connection

- Being Present

9 ELEMENTS DAILY DIARY

Use this diary to help create more awareness of how you are feeling throughout the 9 days, and to see how practicing the different elements affects how you feel.

DAY 1

How do you feel today, before Exercise?

Fantastic

Good

OK

Not Good

Rubbish

Score your feeling out of 10

Balance – do you feel you need more/less/about right today?

Momentum – do you feel you need more/less/about right?

How do you feel today after Exercise?

Fantastic

Good

OK

Not Good

Rubbish

Score your feeling out of 10

What is the best thing that happened to you today?

Exercise reduces frustration, anger, stress, and depression, and creates more Balance in your life.

DAY 2

How do you feel today, before Exercise and Personal Space?

Fantastic

Good

OK

Not Good

Rubbish

Score your feeling out of 10

1. Exercise
2. Personal Space

Balance – do you feel you need more/less/about right today?

Momentum – do you feel you need more/less/about right?

How do you feel today, after Exercise and Personal Space?

Fantastic

Good

OK

Not Good

Rubbish

Score your feeling out of 10

1. Exercise
2. Personal Space

What is the best thing that happened to you today?

Personal Space creates calmness, clarity, reduces stress, reduces frustration, creates presence and awareness.

DAY 3

How do you feel today, before Exercise, Personal Space, and Sleep?

> Fantastic
>
> Good
>
> OK
>
> Not Good
>
> Rubbish

Score your feeling out of 10

1. Exercise
2. Personal Space
3. Sleep

Balance – do you feel you need more/less/about right today?

Momentum – do you feel you need more/less/about right?

How do you feel today, after Exercise, Personal Space, and Sleep?

> Fantastic
>
> Good
>
> OK

Not Good

Rubbish

Score your feeling out of 10

1. Exercise
2. Personal Space
3. Sleep

What is the best thing that happened to you today?

Sleep creates clarity and awareness, it helps focus, reduces irritability and reactive comments, and creates more emotional Balance.

DAY 4

How do you feel today, before Exercise, Personal Space, Sleep, and Nutrition?

Fantastic

Good

OK

Not Good

Rubbish

Score your feeling out of 10

1. Exercise
2. Personal Space
3. Sleep
4. Nutrition

Balance – do you feel you need more/less/about right today?

Momentum – do you feel you need more/less/about right?

How do you feel today, after Exercise, Personal Space, Sleep, and Nutrition?

Fantastic

Good

OK

Not Good

Rubbish

Score your feeling out of 10

1. Exercise
2. Personal Space
3. Sleep
4. Nutrition

What is the best thing that happened to you today?

Nutrition fuels your cells, reduces irritability, increases clarity, and creates more Balance in your life.

DAY 5

How do you feel today, before Exercise, Personal Space, Sleep, Nutrition, and Environment?

Fantastic

Good

OK

Not Good

Rubbish

Score your feeling out of 10

1. Exercise
2. Personal Space

3. Sleep
4. Nutrition
5. Environment

Balance – do you feel you need more/less/about right today?
Momentum – do you feel you need more/less/about right?

How do you feel today, after Exercise, Personal Space, Sleep, Nutrition, and Environment?

Fantastic
Good
OK
Not Good
Rubbish

Score your feeling out of 10

1. Exercise
2. Personal Space
3. Sleep
4. Nutrition
5. Environment

What is the best thing that happened to you today?

Environment reduces stress and depression, and creates either more Balance or Momentum in your life.

DAY 6

How do you feel today, before Exercise, Personal Space, Sleep, Nutrition, Environment, and Achieve and Complete?

Fantastic

Good

OK

Not Good

Rubbish

Score your feeling out of 10

1. Exercise
2. Personal Space
3. Sleep
4. Nutrition
5. Environment
6. Achieve and Complete

Balance – do you feel you need more/less/about right today?

Momentum – do you feel you need more/less/about right?

How do you feel today, after Exercise, Personal Space, Sleep, Nutrition, Environment, and Achieve and Complete?

Fantastic

Good

OK

Not Good

Rubbish

Score your feeling out of 10

1. Exercise
2. Personal Space
3. Sleep
4. Nutrition
5. Environment
6. Achieve and Complete

What is the best thing that happened to you today?

Achieve and Complete increases the feeling of being alive, and creates more Momentum in your life.

DAY 7

How do you feel today, before Exercise, Personal Space, Sleep, Nutrition, Environment, Achieve and Complete, and Learn?

> Fantastic
>
> Good
>
> OK
>
> Not Good
>
> Rubbish

Score your feeling out of 10

1. Exercise
2. Personal Space
3. Sleep
4. Nutrition
5. Environment
6. Achieve and Complete
7. Learn

Balance – do you feel you need more/less/about right today?

Momentum – do you feel you need more/less/about right?

How do you feel today, after Exercise, Personal Space, Sleep, Nutrition, Environment, Achieve and Complete, and Learn?

Fantastic

Good

OK

Not Good

Rubbish

Score your feeling out of 10

1. Exercise
2. Personal Space
3. Sleep
4. Nutrition
5. Environment
6. Achieve and Complete
7. Learn

What is the best thing that happened to you today?

Learn creates more Momentum in your life.

DAY 8

How do you feel today, before Exercise, Personal Space, Sleep, Nutrition, Environment, Achieve and Complete, Learn, and Social Connection?

Fantastic

Good

OK

Not Good

Rubbish

Score your feeling out of 10

1. Exercise
2. Personal Space
3. Sleep
4. Nutrition
5. Environment
6. Achieve and Complete
7. Learn
8. Social Connection

Balance – do you feel you need more/less/about right today?

Momentum – do you feel you need more/less/about right?

How do you feel today, after Exercise, Personal Space, Sleep, Nutrition, Environment, Achieve and Complete, Learn, and Social Connection?

Fantastic

Good

OK

Not Good

Rubbish

Score your feeling out of 10

1. Exercise
2. Personal Space
3. Sleep
4. Nutrition
5. Environment
6. Achieve and Complete
7. Learn
8. Social Connection

What is the best thing that happened to you today?

Social Connection creates more Momentum in your life.

DAY 9

How do you feel today, before Exercise, Personal Space, Sleep, Nutrition, Environment, Achieve and Complete, Learn, Social Connection, and Being Present?

Fantastic

Good

OK

Not Good

Rubbish

Score your feeling out of 10

1. Exercise
2. Personal Space
3. Sleep
4. Nutrition
5. Environment
6. Achieve and Complete
7. Learn
8. Social Connection
9. Being Present

Balance – do you feel you need more/less/about right today?

Momentum – do you feel you need more/less/about right?

Being Present – have you experienced the present moment today? Yes/no?

How do you feel today, after Exercise, Personal Space, Sleep, Nutrition, Environment, Achieve and Complete, Learn, Social Connection, and Being Present?

Fantastic

Good

OK

Not Good

Rubbish

Score your feeling out of 10

1. Exercise
2. Personal Space
3. Sleep
4. Nutrition
5. Environment
6. Achieve and Complete
7. Learn
8. Social Connection
9. Being Present

What is the best thing that happened to you today?

Being Present creates more wholeness in your life.

THE WAY TEACHINGS

To read more about The Way and the 9 Elements, and how they can help you in life, we update the following Web and social media channels regularly:

 Website: http://thewayjohnwhiteman.com

 Facebook: http://facebook.com/thewayjohnwhiteman

 YouTube: thewaybyjohnwhiteman

 Twitter: twitter@johnwhiteman

ASK JOHN

If you have a question for John please contact askjohn@ johnwhiteman.com. John will reply by way of a post or article, so one person's question can open up the probability of helping more people who are experiencing a similar situation.

A NOTE FROM JOHN

Words cannot describe how blessed I am to have such a wonderful wife and two gorgeous sons. When I first mentioned that I wanted to speak and write about my work and experiences they were so supportive; it was amazing.

Doing something new, with absolutely no idea where this decision will take you, is something we do in lesser or greater degrees every day. My decision to speak and write about The Way was taken with a knowing inside of me that this was the right path to take, as I have an inner yearning to help as many people as possible in my life. This book has provided me with a way of fulfilling this dream.

My message is simple: when you break everything down into little pieces, it is easier to understand. With this same process in mind, writing *9 Days To Feel Fantastic* has been a series of small steps that have simply taken me forward to today.

I would very much like to thank my wife, Collette, who helped me to write this book. She has such a lovely way of moving my words around to make them Flow and, without a doubt, it would have been much harder and less enjoyable without her help, dedication, and love; we are a great partnership.

Thank you Collette x

I remember walking along a beach on the South Coast of England, talking with Collette about this next chapter of our lives. We discussed how important it was for us to fulfill our lives and completely live the way that we were teaching others to do. We dreamed of doing something that we both would really love to do, which is to share what my work had revealed with as many people as possible, so we can help a lot more. With this dream in our hearts, we thought how wonderful it would be to have The Way published by Hay House, so I could speak around the world delivering my message.

I am now writing this knowing that our dream is about to become a reality. Thank you, every one of you – you have helped this dream to come true ☺

I pinch myself sometimes when I look out into the world and see how much it has to offer us, while accepting that, at times, we can all experience things that make us feel that life is a chore. I am so happy to be sharing the 9 Elements with you, knowing that many of my clients and I have successfully used them as a way to Feeling Fantastic. My hope is that you, too, will use them and feel this way.

I welcome your feedback.

Thank you, take care, and most of all, I hope you enjoy this book as much as I have enjoyed sharing my message with you.

John x